Choosing A Psychotherapist: A Guide to Navigating The Mental Health Maze

Choosing A Psychotherapist: A Guide to Navigating The Mental Health Maze

Dr. Matthew S. Zimmerman & Dr. Donna Volpe Strouse

Writers Club Press
San Jose New York Lincoln Shanghai

Choosing A Psychotherapist: A Guide to Navigating The Mental
Health Maze

Writers Club Press
an imprint of iUniverse, Inc.

For information address:
iUniverse, Inc.
5220 S. 16th St., Suite 200
Lincoln, NE 68512
www.iuniverse.com

ISBN: 0-595-21910-1

Printed in the United States of America

CONTENTS

ACKNOWLEDGEMENTS

We would like to thank the many people involved in the editing and refining of the material in this book. We owe much gratitude to our "target sample" of editors who tore apart the first version of the book: James Strouse, Catherine Bramlage, Dan Zimmerman, Debbie and Matt Hogan, Patricia Volpe, and Shelley Garraway.

We would also like to thank those who generously contributed information regarding their respective institutions and fields, including Peter Mudd and Kate Nicholas of the International Association for Analytic Psychology, Drs. Leon Hoffman and Ellen Rowntree of the American Psychoanalytic Association, and representatives from the Accreditation Council for Graduate Medical Education. We express our appreciation to the American Psychological Association, the Commission on Accreditation for Marriage and Family Therapy Education, the Council for Accreditation of Counseling and Related Educational Programs, the Council on Social Work Education, the National Council for Accreditation of Teacher Education, and the National League for Nursing Accrediting Commission for also providing useful and timely information.

Finally, we would like to thank other family and friends who supported us along the way, particularly Jack Volpe, John and Jean Volpe, Chris and Scott Ramsey, George and Lois Strouse, Alan and Lori Zimmerman, Honora Zimmerman, Liz Zimmerman, Rebecca Roberts, Dr. Laura and Ted Flynn, Warren Nakatani, P.J. and Amy O'Toole, Dr. Lori and Dennis Pappas, Jillian Peterson, and Carrie Ricci.

CHAPTER 1: INTRODUCTION

The stigma of psychotherapy is dying rapidly, and the notion that only "crazy" people go to therapy is out-dated. In fact, many people go to therapy for self-awareness and personal growth, as well as problems such as feeling depressed, anxious or lonely. Still, many people have unhelpful or "bad" first experiences with a psychotherapist, and you may have as well. It is our belief that the majority of unhelpful therapy experiences are the result of poor matching between therapist and client, and that these can be reduced by both knowing what to look for, and how to find it. There are many factors essential to making a good match between you and a therapist, including:

- What is the training of this psychotherapist?
- Does s(he) come from a school that is accredited by a national board?
- Will the therapist you choose have experience with the issues or problems you bring to therapy?
- Do you want group, individual, family, child or couples psychotherapy?
- How do you work out a payment fee?
- How can you see your psychotherapist for as many sessions as you and your therapist feel are needed, regardless of your insurance's limitations?
- How can you expect your psychotherapist to approach you in treatment?
- How will your psychotherapist help you?
- How does this psychotherapist envision or approach psychological problems?

This guide will help you answer these questions. Whether you are a member of an HMO, PPO, have private insurance, or none at all, you have choices regarding your mental health care. This is particularly true

1

when choosing a psychotherapist. Certainly an HMO may give you a list of psychotherapists to choose from. So how will you make that choice? Assessing your needs is an important step in the process.

Who practices psychotherapy?

You may be confused about who practices psychotherapy and what kind of therapy will be helpful to you. That confusion is well founded. While researching this book, we looked in the phone book under "psychologist," "counselor," and "psychotherapist" and found a variety of descriptive abbreviations for such providers. The following list includes a sample of those abbreviations:

CAC: Certified Addictions Counselor
CGP: Certified Group Psychotherapist
Ed.D.: Doctor of Education
L.I.C.S.W.: Licensed Clinical Social Worker
L.M.H.C.: Licensed Mental Health Counselor
M.A.: Master of Arts
M.D.: Doctor of Medicine
D.O.: Doctor of Osteopathic Medicine
M.Ed.: Master of Education
MFT, LMFT: (Licensed) Marriage and Family Therapist
M.S.: Master of Science
M.S.W.: Master of Social Work
NCSP: Nationally Certified School Psychologist
Ph.D.: Doctor of Philosophy
Psy.D.: Doctor of Psychology
R.N.: Registered Nurse
Th.D.: Doctor of Theology

The following were abbreviations we did not recognize, but a few guesses are provided for you.

CS: In this instance we called the secretary for the nurse who lists herself as *MS RN CS, Certified Clinical Nurse Specialist* and identified ourselves as clients looking for a therapist. We asked what these abbreviations meant, and informed her that we already knew what MS and RN stood for but were stuck with the CS. She replied "I don't know, maybe Certified Specialist?" This may mean her specialty is in certification or that she is certified in having a specialty. Actually, we discovered the true meaning— Clinical Specialist (or Clinical Nurse Specialist in some states).

Our favorite abbreviation was G.Ed. We were most surprised by this one because we were almost sure you could not practice psychotherapy with only a high school diploma (Graduate Equivalence Degree). We inquired about this individual's background as an "interested consumer." To our relief, he was not advertising his high school diploma, nor did he have a degree in Genius of Education (G.Ed.). It was rather a typo made by the phone company. He really had an M.Ed. and his name was Ged. Apparently the phone company was confused by the multitude of abbreviations, as you may have been as well, and could not keep them straight. *So, be cautious of what you read in an advertisement and do not assume what an abbreviation means.* Pay close attention to the abbreviations, because one letter could change your life. You may be looking to join a group to quit smoking (C.G.P.—Certified Group Psychotherapist) and unwittingly end up getting your taxes done instead (that's C.F.P. for Certified Financial Planner).

Do you need psychotherapy?

You must answer this for yourself, but here are some suggestions we have provided for you. You might consider psychotherapy if:

- You are suffering.
- You are having trouble at work, home, school or in the community due to your thoughts, behaviors or feelings.
- You feel as though others are negatively affected by your behavior.
- Others around you are seriously suggesting that you "talk to someone."

- You are experiencing most others as irritating, anxiety provoking or angering.
- You are having trouble letting go of certain ideas, feelings or people.
- You feel alone, isolated or alienated.
- You feel you want to talk to someone with experience in mental health issues for advice or get some information about a particular life situation.
- Your relationships are troubled or not working due to your thoughts, feelings or behaviors.
- You are having thoughts of hurting yourself or someone else. (**If this is the case, it is *highly* recommended to seek professional support immediately.**)

Any one of these is a valid reason for you to seek psychotherapy. However, this is not an exhaustive list. These are only a few reasons that may lead you to talk with a psychotherapist. These indicators also apply to children, so if you are a parent seeking therapy for your child, feel free to use this as a guideline. The ultimate tool for assessing your need for psychotherapy is your own sense and intuition.

The worksheet provided below is to help you clarify your needs and areas of difficulty. It will be particularly useful to you in conjunction with Chapter 7, as you begin the actual process of interviewing prospective psychotherapists. It is recommended that you complete the worksheet before continuing.

Problem Worksheet

Use this worksheet to help you get a clear idea of what your problem areas may be, and how they affect various aspects of your life. This will be particularly useful to you after you have read about training, credentialing, theoretical orientation, type of therapy and subspecialties in upcoming chapters.

1. *What are the problem(s) for which you are seeking psychotherapy?*
2. *What thoughts, feelings and behaviors are associated with it?*
3. *How do those thoughts, feelings and behaviors cause pain or suffering for you?*
4. *What is your understanding of how your problem(s) developed and how it/they are maintained?*
5. *How does it affect your relationships with partners, friends, family and coworkers?*
6. *What do others think of your problem? Is it more of a problem for you or others?*
7. *How does it affect your ability to perform in your occupation?*
8. *How long has it been a problem? Is it a recurring problem? If so, how often does it recur? If it is an enduring problem, can you recall a time when you did not struggle with it?*
9. *Have you ever been in therapy before? If so, was it for the same problem? What was helpful previously and what was not?*
10. *What are you hoping to get from therapy? How would your thoughts, feelings, behavior and/or interpersonal relationships be different?*
11. *How long do you expect to work on your problem in therapy? Is this realistic?*
12. *What are some issues, concerns or logistics that may get in the way of an effective therapy experience for you?*
13. *If you have never been in therapy, what are your expectations about it?*
14. *What are your reservations about its effectiveness or ability to help you, if any?*

Previous Therapy Worksheet

This worksheet will help you identify aspects of your previous therapy experience that were beneficial and those that were not. It will also be helpful for you clarify how your current situation and needs differ from when you were in therapy previously. Use this worksheet in conjunction with the Problem Worksheet, as well as the information in the book on theoretical orientation, type of therapy, and subspecialty areas to better match yourself with a therapist.

1. *How do the problems for which you are seeking therapy now differ from the problems for which you sought therapy in the past?*
2. *What was most helpful in your previous therapy (list 3)? Why was each helpful?*
3. *Would your current difficulties be better handled similarly or differently from your previous therapy?*
4. *Were you satisfied with your previous therapist's skill level? If not, what would have been more helpful for you?*
5. *What questions did you ask of your previous therapist before beginning? What questions do you wish you had asked?*
6. *Are you looking for a therapist to approach you similarly, or are you looking for a different approach? (Refer to Chapter 4 for detailed information of theoretical approaches)*
7. *If your problem is recurring, would you be more comfortable with the therapist who knows you better?*
8. *What are you hoping to get from therapy this time and how does that differ from your previous goals and expectations?*
9. *If your previous therapy was less successful, what will you do to contribute to making your therapy experience more beneficial for you?*
10. *What qualities of your previous therapist were comfortable and/or helpful to you? (i.e., gender, religion, shared interests)*

11. What qualities of your previous therapist were less comfortable and/or helpful to you?

12. Use the space provided below to take additional notes on how the answers to these questions clarify what you are currently seeking in a psychotherapist.

Not everyone feels the need for psychotherapy, and there are many other sources of support that are recommended. These include family, friends, clergy or pastors, teachers and guidance counselors, advisors, and even hairdressers. These sources of support are in no way mutually exclusive with psychotherapy. In fact, most psychotherapists recognize the importance of multiple sources of support, and will recommend seeking out such sources while actively engaged in psychotherapy.

Qualities specific to psychotherapy

There are many advantages to seeking psychotherapy. Some of these overlap from what could be provided by clergy or a friend, but many others are unique to psychotherapy. While having someone simply listen is a common means of support, psychotherapy differs in that the therapist is trained to listen in a much more in-depth way. For instance, when a client shares with a friend her difficulties in a romantic relationship, the friend will listen (hopefully) and perhaps give some advice. The psychotherapist, on the other hand, is likely hypothesizing about the nature of all of this person's romantic relationships, as well as how her history contributes to her way of relating. These are only hypotheses to be confirmed and not assumptions.

Psychotherapy is also a place where the client can experience positive regard from the therapist, regardless of particular behaviors in which the person is engaged. A basic assumption for psychotherapists is that to help a person, the therapist must understand why the person is behaving that way (there are a few exceptions to this). Behaviors such as bingeing/purging, excessive masturbation, and even domestic violence are examples of those the therapist will try to understand. This does not mean the therapist will condone the behaviors. In fact, battering must be reported if involving a minor, disabled or elderly person, and the client should be told that up-front by the therapist. Nevertheless, the therapist will want to understand the person engaged in that behavior, so that s(he) can be understood and helped.

This leads to another essential component common to all psychotherapy—empathy. Empathy is the experience of feeling another's feelings and has an "as-if" quality. This means that the therapist attempts to experience what the client is sharing "as-if" the therapist was the client. Another way to think about empathy is the therapist's attempt to "walk in the client's shoes." This is both a natural characteristic of a particular therapist, and something that can be refined through training. Empathy fosters genuine connections between any two people, including a therapist and client. Of course there is the understanding that one person is the therapist and one the client, but in some respect that is irrelevant to the experience of empathic understanding.

Another factor special but not necessarily unique to psychotherapy is that of a one-way relationship. The client does not need to be concerned with the feelings or thoughts of the therapist, although he or she may be interested and is welcome to ask. The client is there to be helped, and there is not a sense of balance between therapist and client regarding sharing of personal information. This makes it different from talking to a friend or family member where there is undoubtedly pressure to consider the other's feelings when talking about your own.

Finally, a psychotherapist is someone with training in how to assess and work with individual personalities. Most therapists adjust to each person, and the ultimate goal of an effective therapist is to learn how a particular person thinks, feels and experiences, so he or she can be better helped. These are only some of the ways psychotherapy will be advantageous to you.

PSYCHOTHERAPIST	OTHER SUPPORTS
Listens more objectively, considering the person's current situation and overall personality	Listens subjectively
Often abstains from advice-giving	Gives advice (possibly based on their own needs)
Displays nonjudgmental understanding	May be quick to judge "unappealing behaviors"
Displays empathic understanding	May or may not be empathic
One-way relationship in which client need not be aware or empathize with therapist's feelings	Two-way relationship in which both members are sensitive to the other's feelings
Trained to work with different personalities and problems	Lack training in diverse personalities and problems

This chart in no way implies that other supports are less valuable. However, we want you to be able to distinguish between therapy and other supports and recognize that therapists have additional skills to offer besides a supportive ear.

What this guidebook offers

This guidebook is intended to provide you with helpful information in your search for a psychotherapist that best fits your needs. Chapters 2 and 3 inform you about the credentialing of psychotherapists. Specifically, Chapter 2 provides descriptions of typical professionals who practice psychotherapy, including information about degrees, training, and work setting. Chapter 3 highlights the importance of accreditation and discusses the accreditation guidelines for various psychotherapy training programs.

Chapters 4, 5, and 6 address the three pillars of psychotherapy: theoretical orientation, types of psychotherapy, and subspecialty areas. Specifically,

Chapter 4 discusses theoretical orientation, or the different ways in which psychotherapists approach individuals and their problems. Chapter 5 describes the various types of psychotherapy that a therapist may practice, such as child, group and couples therapy. Chapter 6 highlights the many subspecialty areas in which psychotherapists may specialize, such as substance abuse, anxiety problems, depression or body image concerns.

Chapters 7 provides specific questions for interviewing prospective psychotherapists, and how to assess whether or not the psychotherapist will be particularly helpful in meeting your needs. These questions are based on information provided in the previous chapters, so it will be helpful for you to refer to them as needed. At the end of Chapter 7, we have included a number of blank questionnaire forms to assist you when interviewing psychotherapists. Chapter 8 lists resources that will be helpful in your search for therapy and support groups.

CHAPTER 2: WHO PROVIDES PSYCHOTHERAPY?

People often wonder who can provide psychotherapy. The list provided in this chapter attempts to answer that question for you. The purpose of this chapter is to cover as many of the people you may find in the phone book calling themselves "psychologists" or "psychotherapists" (and they are numerous). We have included information about degrees, training, and what these psychotherapists do on a daily basis. Historically, the primary disciplines that engaged in therapy were psychologists, psychiatrists, and social workers. More recently however, there has been an increase in the number of Master's level practitioners who provide therapy, in addition to alternative disciplines, such as nursing.

Most of the training requirements included in this chapter are based on those programs accredited by their profession's accrediting body. Chapter 3 gives an overview of the accreditation for the most common training programs for psychotherapists. So keep in mind that the training requirements listed in this chapter represent *accredited* programs only. Some information about licensing and certification is also included, and what it means to be licensed or certified. Usually, there are certain requirements one must meet before they can sit for the licensing or certification exam (which is similar to the bar exam that lawyers must pass to be called "attorneys"). To give an example, we will illustrate the requirements for a licensed clinical psychologist. Someone in training to become a licensed clinical psychologist in the state of Massachusetts, for example, must complete his or her doctorate in clinical psychology with an additional year of clinical experience supervised by a licensed clinical psychologist. Candidates take a licensing exam once these requirements are met. Those who pass can refer to themselves as "licensed clinical psychologists."

Failing the licensing exam does not necessarily exclude a doctoral-level practitioner from providing services or getting a decent job. Licensing and certification requirements vary from state to state, even within the same discipline. For example, in many states a Master's degree in psychology is sufficient for licensure. And in some states, a doctoral degree is not required to call oneself a "psychologist." Some states do not require a license at all, depending on the profession. However, insurance reimbursement is usually predicated on licensure or certification.

This notion is important because a psychotherapist who is not licensed or certified (in a state requiring licensure) does not have that state's "stamp of approval." The purpose of states licensing practitioners is to protect the public by attempting to establish a level of competency and ethical practice.

Professionals who may work as psychotherapists include (but are not limited to):

• Psychologists

• Social Workers

• Psychiatrists

• Psychoanalysts

• Jungian Analysts

• Marriage and Family Therapists

• Counselors

• Master's Level Clinicians

• Advanced Practice Nurses

• Clergy

The descriptions on Psychoanalysis and Jungian Analysis represent *examples* of training for psychoanalysts and Jungian analysts, respectively. There are a multitude of training institutes for each, as well as other types of analytic training. For our description, we have chosen the most common types of analysts and two of the largest national accrediting organizations. The information described in the examples provided here is particular to the American Psychoanalytic Association (APsaA) and the International Association for Analytical Psychology (IAAP).

PSYCHOLOGISTS

- *Degree*: Ph.D., Psy.D., or Ed.D.
- *Accrediting Body*: APA (American Psychological Association) or NCATE (National Council for Accreditation of Teacher Education, in association with NASP—National Association of School Psychologists)

Who are they?

The work of psychologists varies depending on their discipline. Clinical psychologists work in a variety of settings, including private practice, hospitals, universities, and mental health clinics. They work with any psychological problem, including depressed or anxious adults, chronic pain patients, war veterans, unhappy couples, children, or college students, just to name a few. Counseling psychologists typically work with students at the university level. Counseling psychologists work with clients on developing their educational and career interests, learning study strategies, and dealing with difficult interpersonal relationships or personal problems. School psychologists work in public or private schools, or in academic or research institutions. They work with students, teachers, parents, administrators, and coaches on how to deal with behavior problems or learning difficulties. On a given day, a psychologist may provide personality or psychological tests, consult with the court system, perform diagnostic interviews, provide individual, group, family or couples psychotherapy, teach a class, or work as an administrator. Most psychologists focus their efforts on one or two specialties, like psychotherapy and assessment, or teaching and administration. Psychologists are the only professionals who are legally permitted to interpret psychological tests in most states.

Training:

Training for a psychologist varies among states and institutions with regard to type, length, and requirements. Primarily, psychologists earn their degree through a university's graduate school of education or psychology or through a professional school of psychology. The length of the training is typically a minimum of 4 years with a maximum length of stay depending on completion of dissertation (original research project). However, the average training is 3-4 years of coursework and practicum training (supervised work in the field) and one year of predoctoral internship (supervised field work usually with more responsibilities than practicum training). The number of practicum training hours varies, as some graduate students have 600 hours of direct client contact (supervised by a licensed clinical psychologist) while others have up to 1,500 hours, thus being better trained for predoctoral internship. Other training requirements include a dissertation or research project and some form of comprehensive exams.

Licensing in most states requires a minimum of predoctoral internship and postdoctoral hours, (approximately 1,600-2,000 hours for each) totaling 3,200-4,000 hours. In several states, school psychologists may also elect to become certified as a Nationally Certified School Psychologist (NCSP) by the National Association of School Psychologists.

Note: Psychologists with a Psy.D. degree often have more training in assessment and therapy than Ph.D.s., while Ph.D.s usually have more training in clinical research. However, many Ph.D.s and Psy.D.s are equally qualified to provide therapy, assessment, or research services, especially those coming from programs in which Ph.D.s and Psy.D.s are trained together.

SOCIAL WORKERS

- *Degree*: M.S.W., LICSW (or LCSW)
- *Accrediting Body*: CSWE (Council on Social Work Education)

Who are they?

Social workers provide therapy or counseling to a wide range of clients in a variety of settings, depending on their specialty. They may work with families, individuals, or groups, and they often provide help with problem-solving, obtaining access to resources, and coping with emotional problems. They usually provide very practical help, such as teaching job skills or helping a family to find housing. Clinical social workers provide psychotherapy and can be found in almost any therapeutic setting, ranging from a university counseling center to private practice to a mental health clinic. Mental health social workers also provide psychotherapy and focus on helping clients adjust to community living and learn daily living skills.

Training:

An M.S.W. is typically offered though a university's department or school of social work. Training for a Master's in social work (if accredited by CSWE) requires two years of full-time academic study with at least 900 hours of field placement. Some programs may require a thesis, comprehensive exams, or internship.

To become a Licensed Clinical Social Worker (LICSW or LCSW), one must get licensed in the state in which they wish to practice. Licensing requirements vary from state to state. Social workers can also elect to be voluntarily certified for various specialties by the National Association of Social Workers (NASP).

Note: We did not mention professionals with Ph.D.s in social work (or D.S.W.—doctor of social work) because they typically do not provide clinical services, but spend their time either teaching or doing administrative work. However, that does not rule out the possibility that you may see someone for therapy who has his or her doctorate in social work. In addition, social workers with their Bachelor's degree in social work (B.S.W.) may also provide therapy, but cannot do so in private practice. Typically they work as case workers and are supervised by LICSW's or LCSW's.

PSYCHIATRISTS

- *Degree*: M.D., D.O.
- *Accrediting Body*: ACGME (Accreditation Council for Graduate Medical Education)

Who are they?

Psychiatrists are medical doctors (hence the M.D.) with a specialty in psychiatry. They may work in a number of different settings, including hospitals, community mental health centers, VA hospitals, private practice, and university counseling centers. On a typical day, they may see clients for individual therapy, evaluate clients for medication and hospitalization, prescribe medication, supervise other therapists, or provide administrative services. You are most likely to see a psychiatrist for therapy in an outpatient setting, like private practice or a university. In a hospital, they more typically provide medication, not therapy. Again, this is not a hard and fast rule—*a psychiatrist in any setting may provide therapy or prescribe medication, but psychiatrists who provide therapy are increasingly rare.*

Training:

Psychiatrists begin their training in medical school, but get the bulk of their psychiatric training during their four-year residency. Residency training varies depending on the program regarding type and length of rotations. Residencies may require rotations in a variety of settings including universities, hospitals, and VA medical centers, working with patients of all ages. Residencies also vary with regard to training in psychotherapy, as some residencies provide a lot of training, while others only focus on medication therapy. For an ACGME-accredited residency, residents may spend 12 of the 48 months in an approved child and adolescent psychiatry residency. The first year of post-graduate psychiatric training (PGY-1) must include a minimum of four months in internal medicine, family practice or pediatrics. The first year cannot include more than 8 months in psychiatry training. The last three years are spent balancing psychiatry education and direct patient care, with a priority held to educational requirements. Following residency, candidates apply for certification by the American Board of Psychiatry and Neurology (ABPN).

PSYCHOANALYSTS

- *Degree*: Post-graduate non-degree program
- *Accrediting Body*: APsaA (American Psychoanalytic Association)

Who are they?

Psychoanalysts (or classical analysts) may work in a variety of settings, including private practice, hospitals, universities, and medical schools. Although historically psychoanalysts have provided long-term psychoanalysis with their patients, managed care has made this a luxury for many as insurance will not typically cover the cost of this treatment. Therefore, those who are interested in attending long-term therapy, two or three times a week, are required to pay out of their own pockets, which limits traditional psychoanalysis to those who have the financial means. However, psychoanalysts will also work with patients on a briefer intensive basis, and many will work with couples, families, and groups. In addition to psychotherapy, they also spend time doing research, supervision, education, and administration.

Training:

Psychoanalysts are either medical doctors who have completed a four-year residency in psychiatry, or professionals who hold their doctorate in either psychology or social work; i.e. M.D., Ph.D., Psy.D., Ed.D., D.S.W. Other qualified candidates may be accepted for training if they hold the highest degree in their field and receive intensive clinical work in mental health. For example, a board-certified physician in dermatology could apply for psychoanalytic training as long as they complete prerequisite training in the mental health field. Psychoanalytic training is post-graduate (i.e., after graduate school). Training as approved by APsaA consists of coursework in psychoanalytic theory and technique, personal analysis, and closely supervised analysis with at least three patients. Psychoanalytic training typically lasts from six to ten years.

JUNGIAN ANALYSTS

- *Degree*: Post-graduate non-degree program
- *Accrediting Body*: IAAP (International Association for Analytical Psychology)

Who are they?

Jungian analysts may look like psychoanalysts on the surface. They may work in the same settings as psychoanalysts, and have typically worked with long-term patients. However, the difference between the two lay primarily with their theoretical beliefs. For more information, see the section on Classical Analysis in Chapter 4.

Training:

Training and background for Jungian analysts vary greatly among institutes, even within the same accrediting organization. For example, some institutes require that candidates be licensed to practice psychotherapy, while others will accept graduate degrees in any discipline. Training under the auspices of IAAP typically requires some number of hours of personal analysis with a certified Jungian analyst, as well as coursework in analytical psychology, dreams, and psychopathology, and closely supervised analysis with their own clients (referred to as "analysands"). Training typically lasts from five to ten years.

MARRIAGE AND FAMILY THERAPISTS

- *Degree*: Ph.D., Psy.D., MMFT, M.S., M.A.
- *Accrediting Body*: COAMFTE (the Commission on Accreditation for Marriage and Family Therapy Education)

Who are they?

Marriage and family therapists (MFT's) work with individuals, couples, and families (their title may be a little misleading). They may work with a number of mental health issues through individual, couples or family therapy, including but not limited to marital distress, alcohol or drug abuse, child behavior problems, eating disorders, or depression. Marriage and family therapists may also practice in a variety of settings from hospitals to private practice to universities. You may see them for therapy in any of these settings.

Training:

The training for a marriage and family therapist is offered through a number of educational settings, including schools of social work, education, psychology, or sociology. The training typically involves a minimum of two years of academic and fieldwork for the Master's degree and four years for the doctoral degree, including internship and dissertation (with a minimum of 500 direct client contact hours).

Certification and licensing requirements for marriage and family therapists vary from state to state. All states that provide licensure require a minimum of a Master's degree and some supervised clinical experience. Some states still do not require a license for practice as a marriage and family therapist.

Note: This description was devoted to MFT's who earned their degree specifically in marriage and family therapy. There are a number of professionals who practice marriage and family therapy who earned their degree in a different field, such as psychology or social work, who have earned their post-graduate degree in marriage and family therapy.

COUNSELORS

- *Degree*: M.S., M.A., M.Ed.
- *Accrediting Body*: CACREP (Council for Accreditation of Counseling and Related Educational Programs)

Who are they?

Counselors may work in a variety of settings, depending on their specialty area. They can be found in schools, colleges, private practice, hospitals, employment agencies, community mental health centers, etc. School and college counselors work in schools and colleges (surprise, surprise) providing a number of services to students related to personal, academic, career, and drug counseling. Mental health counselors provide psychotherapy to help clients deal with a variety of mental health issues, including family problems, substance abuse, and depression. Substance abuse counselors work specifically with substance abusers and may provide individual or group counseling to help deal with the addiction. Marriage and family counselors work primarily with families and couples. Career counselors provide services related to career exploration and career development. Counselors may also specialize in a particular area such as multicultural counseling. You may see any one of these counselors for therapy, depending on your presenting problem (or initial reason for seeking therapy).

Training:

Master's level counselors are typically trained through a university's department of education or psychology. Training usually requires one to two years of academic and clinical experience in counseling. Some programs also require some type of a thesis or research project. The training varies between schools and depends on the specific focus of the counseling degree (whether it is mental health, school, community, etc.). For programs accredited by CACREP, training involves a minimum of 48 to 60 semester hours of academic work, 100 hours of supervised practicum, and 600 hours of supervised internship.

Most states also have some form of licensing or certification. Not surprisingly, requirements vary from state to state: in some states, counselors may practice independently of another's supervision (such as an LMHC—licensed mental health counselor), while other states require the doctoral degree for independent practice. Counselors can also elect to be certified as a "National Certified Counselor" by the National Board for Certified Counselors (NBCC).

MASTER'S LEVEL CLINICIANS
(Master's in Clinical Psychology)

- *Degree*: M.S. or M.A.
- *Accrediting Body*: None (APA only accredits doctoral programs)

Who are they?

Master's level clinicians may provide therapy, perform evaluations, conduct research, or teach, but in many states only under the supervision of a doctoral level psychologist. They can be found in a variety of settings, including private practice, hospitals, universities, and community mental health centers.

Training:

Training is usually provided through a university's department of psychology or education. Requirements typically include two years of academic and practical experience in addition to a Master's thesis or research project. In some states, Master's level clinicians are eligible to become licensed and work in private practice, which would demand additional training requirements beyond the Master's education. On the other hand, most states will certify school psychologists with a Master's degree upon completion of an internship. The majority of these Master's level programs are housed within a doctoral program, so many of these students are actually working towards their doctorate. However, some of these programs are "terminal", i.e. the Master's degree indicates completion of a program.

ADVANCED PRACTICE NURSES

(either Nurse Practitioner or Clinical Specialist)

- *Degree*: MSN, MS, or ARNP (with additional certification)
- *Accrediting Body*: NLNAC (National League for Nursing Accrediting Commission)

Who are they?

The two types of advanced practice nurses who may provide therapy are nurse practitioners and clinical nurse specialists. Both can provide therapy (either individual or group) independently of another's supervision and can bill insurance for their services. Nurse practitioners typically work in outpatient settings when providing therapy services, and can prescribe limited medication in some states. Clinical nurse specialists may work in a variety of settings including private, inpatient, and health clinics. Nurses, due to their medical training, often work with the chronically mentally ill, patients with combined medical and psychiatric histories, or perform crisis evaluations. However, advanced practice nurses can work with a variety of populations, depending on their training and specialization in graduate school. You would most likely see a nurse practitioner or clinical nurse specialist for therapy in private practice or mental health clinics.

Training:

Advanced nurse practitioners are typically trained through a university's graduate nursing program, and are often times based at medical school teaching hospitals. Both nurse practitioners and clinical nurse specialists earn their Master's degrees in addition to becoming certified in their specialty area upon graduation. A typical training program requires a minimum of one to two years of academic, practical, and research training. Following the Master's degree, advanced practice nurses are required to become certified or licensed in their specialty area in the state they wish to practice.

Note: In this chapter we only focused on nurses who you *may* find in the phone book when looking under "psychotherapist". Many advanced practice nurses do not provide therapy at all, but rather offer more medical services. In addition, there are other nurses who may provide therapy as part of their daily activities (like R.N.s or L.P.N.s), but only in an inpatient setting. Therefore, one would not likely seek their services for outpatient therapy. In addition, there are also professionals with Ph.D.s in nursing, but they usually administrate, teach, or engage in research, and do not often work as psychotherapists.

CLERGY

- *Degree*: Varied (See below)
- *Accrediting Body:* A Higher Power (there is an American Association for Pastoral Counselors that represents and establishes professional guidelines for some clergy)

Who are they?

Ministers, pastors, priests, rabbis and other clergy perform a number of different tasks, including delivering sermons, providing solace, presiding over funerals, absolving sins, marrying couples, and counseling those in need. Many clergy provide counseling to their congregation on a variety of issues, particularly marital difficulties, addictions, and spiritual conflicts. Chaplains also work through the university setting to provide counseling to students.

Training:

The training of these professionals varies greatly and depends on their religious backgrounds. Some have advanced degrees and some do not; some have training in counseling and some do not; and some may give a biased view because of their religious beliefs while others may be able to provide a more neutral viewpoint. In fact, some clergy have graduate degrees in psychotherapy in addition to their religious training. There are some institutions that accredit pastoral counselors, however it is not necessary for a member of the clergy to be accredited in order to provide services. The best advice we have is to check these resources for yourself if you are seeking more spiritual or religious counseling.

To summarize the information in this chapter, we have included this easy reference chart for your convenience.

PSYCHOTHERAPIST	DEGREE(S)	ACCREDITING BODY
Psychologist	Ph.D., Psy.D., Ed.D.	APA, NCATE
Social Worker	M.S.W., LICSW, LCSW	CSWE
Psychiatrist	M.D., D.O.	ACGME
Psychoanalyst	M.D., Ph.D., Psy.D., Ed.D., D.S.W.	APsaA (one example)
Jungian Analyst	Varies	IAAP (one example)
Marriage and Family Therapist	Ph.D., Psy.D., MMFT, M.S., M.A.	COAMFTE
Counselor	M.S., M.A., M.Ed.	CACREP
Master's Level Clinician	M.S., M.A.	None
Advanced Practice Nurse	MSN or MS with additional certification	NLNAC
Clergy	Varies	Varies

CHAPTER 3: ACCREDITING BODIES AND WHY THEY EXIST

"Accreditation is a system for recognizing educational institutions and professional programs affiliated with those institutions for a level of performance, integrity, and quality which entitles them to the confidence of the educational community and the public they serve. In the United States this recognition is extended primarily through nongovernmental, voluntary institutional or professional associations. These groups establish criteria for accreditation, arrange site visits, and evaluate those institutions and professional programs which desire accredited status, and publicly designate those which meet their criteria.

"Specialized accreditation of professional and occupational schools and programs is granted by commissions on accreditation set up by national professional organizations in such fields as business, dentistry, engineering, and law. Each of these groups has its distinctive definitions of eligibility, criteria for accreditation, and operating procedures, but *all have undertaken accreditation activities, primarily to provide quality assurances concerning educational preparation of members of the profession or occupation.*" (Commission on Recognition of Postsecondary Accreditation; as cited in APA, 1996)

In other words, accrediting bodies evaluate educational institutions and training programs and set the standards they feel are necessary in grooming quality professionals. They establish the criteria that are necessary (but not necessarily sufficient) to produce competent, caring professionals.

The purpose of this chapter is to introduce accrediting institutions to you: who they are, what they do, and why they are important. You will be provided only with those accrediting bodies that govern the institutions that produce psychotherapists.

Information on accreditation is important for several reasons. One of the most important functions accrediting bodies serve is to designate ethical guidelines for professionals to follow. This is essential because it protects you, the consumer, and prevents you from potential exploitation (e.g., psychotherapists cannot have intimate relationships with their clients). Many of these guidelines have been based on the notion that the therapeutic relationship is not an equal one, given that therapists often are aware of their client's vulnerabilities while the reverse is not true. This inequality in the relationship puts the therapist in a unique and powerful position, which should only be used in helping the client overcome his or her issues. However, there is also the risk of exploitation. For example, a sexual relationship between therapist and client is not viewed as healthy because it can never be equal, and it puts the client at risk for exploitation. If you should have a concern that your psychotherapist is responsible for an ethical violation, please contact the state licensing board or board of professional regulation (if the offender is a licensed professional), or the appropriate accrediting institution, national or state organization listed in the resources chapter (chapter 7).

Another function of accrediting bodies is to ensure quality of training of professionals. The example of the American Psychological Association illustrates why this information is important to you. In training for a clinical psychologist, both training programs and internship sites are accredited by the APA. A psychologist may have attended an accredited training program and a non-accredited internship site, or vice-versa (though much less likely because APA-accredited internship sites are highly competitive and many require accredited doctoral training for eligibility). Another scenario is that a psychologist has attended both a non-accredited training program and non-accredited internship site. Such practitioners do not have the APA's "stamp of approval." This is not to say that someone trained in a non-accredited site will make a poor therapist, nor will all therapists trained at APA-accredited sites be terrific. It is, however, a distinction about which you have a right to know, and may speak to the quality of your therapist. There are many people calling themselves psychotherapists with little or no training in psychotherapy, and who are not bound to the guidelines of an accrediting body. In fact, in many states anyone can put out a shingle and call themselves a "psychotherapist" without being in violation of the law, as long as they do not portray themselves as a "psychologist," "psychiatrist," etc. Therefore, you can see why it is important to know a little bit about someone's training. Would you want someone performing heart transplant surgery on you that has not attended medical school, or is not recognized by the American Medical Association (AMA) as a surgeon? We recommend that you be as protective of your psyche as you are of your heart. Do not let your ego fall into the wrong hands.

The remainder of this chapter is devoted to identifying the various accrediting bodies that accredit training programs for potential psychotherapists, followed by a brief summary of each psychotherapy group's accrediting guidelines. The following list may not be exhaustive—we did our best to include those organizations that represent the largest numbers of psychotherapists in their respective fields. The accrediting bodies and the programs they accredit are broken down in the following table:

ACCREDITING INSTITUTION	*PROGRAM TYPE*
Accreditation Council for Graduate Medical Education (ACGME)	Psychiatry Residencies
American Psychological Association (APA)	Clinical, Counseling, and School Psychology (Doctoral programs only)
Commission on Accreditation for Marriage and Family Therapy Education (COAMFTE)	Marriage and Family therapy (Master's or Doctoral programs)
Council for Accreditation of Counseling and Related Educational Programs (CACREP)	Master's programs in counseling
Council on Social Work Education (CSWE)	Social Work (Bachelor's or Master's)
National Council for Accreditation of Teacher Education (NCATE)	School Psychology offered through School of Education (Master's or Doctoral programs)
National League for Nursing Accrediting Commission (NLNAC)	Nursing Programs (Associate's, Bachelor's or Master's programs)

Accreditation Council for Graduate Medical Education (ACGME)

Psychiatry residency programs are accredited by the ACGME through a peer-review process. The Psychiatry Residency Review Committee (RRC) is the committee within the ACGME responsible for approving psychiatry residencies. The RRC is made up of professionals from three sponsoring organizations: the American Medical Association (AMA), American Psychiatric Association (APA), and the American Board of Psychiatry and Neurology (ABPN). In order for a psychiatry residency to be accredited by ACGME, it must be at least 4 years in length (one of which could be spent in child and adolescent psychiatry residency). The first year of training must include at least 4 months in a different rotation (either internal medicine, pediatrics, or family practice). The next three years of training combines thorough education in clinical psychiatry with direct patient care and supervision (i.e., practice under the direction of a licensed or more experienced professional). (ACGME, 1995)

American Psychological Association (APA)

The APA (not to be confused with the other APA for psychiatrists) is the governing body for practicing psychologists in the U.S. that has developed a set of standards for the training of psychologists. In order for a doctoral training program to be "APA-accredited" (the APA only accredits doctoral programs in either clinical, counseling, or school psychology), it must meet the minimum standards set forth in their guidelines. A training program must offer doctoral education and training in psychology, be sponsored by a nationally accredited institution of higher education, require a minimum of 3 years full-time graduate academic study, and one year of predoctoral internship (to be completed in 1-2 years) in order for the training program to be eligible for accreditation. These are just the basic requirements. To list them all would require eighteen pages and would likely bore you to tears. (APA, 1996)

Commission on Accreditation for Marriage and Family Therapy Education (COAMFTE)

The COAMFTE (a division of the American Association for Marriage and Family Therapy) accredits marriage and family therapy training programs at the Master's, doctoral, and post-graduate levels. In order to be accredited by COAMFTE, a program must meet the six standard curriculum didactic area requirements (teaching topics). These include 1) theoretical foundations, 2) Clinical practice, 3) Individual development and family relations, 4) Professional identity and ethics, 5) Research, and 6) Additional learning (although the degree to which they are provided varies from program to program). In addition, doctoral programs must provide curricula related to clinical supervision, research, dissertation, and clinical practica and internship. Master's programs are a minimum of 2 years, while doctoral programs are a minimum of four. Doctoral programs require a minimum of 500 client hours (250 of which must be relational—couples or families) and 100 hours of supervision. (COAMFTE, 1997)

Council for Accreditation of Counseling and Related Educational Programs (CACREP)

CACREP was formed as a corporate affiliate of the American Counseling Association (ACA). CACREP accredits Master's level counseling programs and doctoral programs in counselor education and supervision, but we will focus on their Master's programs because they are the ones who typically provide psychotherapy (those with doctorates typically teach). CACREP accredits programs in counselor education, community (with specializations in career and gerontological counseling), mental health, school, student affairs, and marriage and family counseling (not to be confused with AAMFT or American Association for Marriage and Family Therapy). To be accredited by CACREP, a program must provide 48 to 60 semester hours of academic work (the former for community and school counseling programs, the latter for mental health and marriage and family therapy counseling). Requirements also include a minimum of 100 hours of supervised practicum and 600 hours of supervised internship (post-practicum). (CACREP, 1994)

Council on Social Work Education (CSWE)

The Commission on Accreditation of the Council on Social Work Education (CSWE) has developed standards that social work education programs must follow in order to be accredited. The Commission accredits at both the Bachelor's and Master's level. However, only Master's level programs will be discussed since persons from these programs are the professionals you may see for therapy. In order for a program to be accredited it must be offered through a nationally accredited college or university and require two years of full-time academic study. The Commission requires a minimum of 900 hours in field practicum with regard to practicum training (supervised social work service). Some of the criteria required by the Commission include that education must prepare individuals to work with diverse populations and clients, teach about ethics and values for practicing professionals, and be based on a liberal arts perspective. These are a few of the most relevant criteria for your purposes of understanding the value of accreditation. In addition to content on social work values and ethics and diversity, Master's level curriculum must include content on social and economic justice, populations-at-risk, human behavior and the social environment, social welfare policy and services, social work practice, research and field practicum. (CSWE, 1994)

National Council for Accreditation of Teacher Education (NCATE)

NCATE accredits school psychology programs at the Master's, post-Master's, specialist, or doctoral level when they are offered through a university's school of education. (As indicated earlier, the American Psychological Association also accredits school psychology programs at the doctoral level). NCATE accredits the schools of education that provide the school psychology training program in conjunction with guidelines set forth by the National Association of School Psychologists (NASP). In order for a school psychology program to be accredited by NCATE it must incorporate knowledge about psychological foundations, educational foundations, interventions and problem solving, statistics and research methodologies, and professional school psychology. The requirements also include closely supervised practica (no specified minimum number of hours) and a year-long internship (at least half of which is completed in a school setting). Doctoral students must complete a minimum of four full-time academic years and one year of internship (a minimum of 1500 hours). (NASP, 1994)

National League for Nursing Accrediting Commission (NLNAC)

The NLNAC accredits post-secondary, Bachelor's and Master's degree nursing programs. You only need to be concerned with Master's level programs that offer degrees in advanced practice nursing because only individuals certified at the Master's level may provide psychotherapy to you. In order for a program to be accredited by the NLN, it must be offered through an accredited institution that is legally authorized to grant the degree, and it must have graduated at least one class. The accreditation guidelines also include a number of criteria incorporating standards for the program's mission, faculty, students, curriculum, resources, educational effectiveness, and creativity. These include the academic and professional qualifications of the faculty, the adequacy of the clinical facilities, and the availability and comprehensiveness of learning resources. (NLNAC, 1997)

You should now have a general understanding of accrediting institutions and what they do, as well as why this information is important to you in choosing a psychotherapist. The next chapter will explain the different therapeutic approaches of psychotherapists.

CHAPTER 4: THEORETICAL ORIENTATION

We have now provided you important information on the issues of accreditation, training and degrees. But now is the fun part—teasing apart psychotherapists by orientation. Here we are referring to theoretical orientation, which refers to the style or approach a psychotherapist uses with a client in therapy. All therapies are grounded in theory, and it is helpful for you to have an understanding of the various psychotherapeutic approaches based on these theories.

Where things stand today

Since the mid-nineteenth century there has been an explosion of psychological theories, including experimental, social, neuropsychological and psychotherapeutic. Even when only discussing various psychotherapy theories, there are over 500 theoretical approaches and more on the way. For example, a book called *The Psychotherapy Handbook: The A to Z Guide to More than 250 Different Therapies in Use Today* (Herink, 1980) describes a multitude of therapies including those referred to as creative aggression therapy, anti-expectation therapy, bio-scream therapy, past lives therapy, photo counseling and radix neo-reichian education. Later on in this book, you will be helped with how to choose a psychotherapist by asking the questions that help determine who is the best "fit" for you, and therefore most able to work well with you as you engage in the process of change and growth.

Most therapists generally belong to some variation of one of the following three major schools of thought:

- *Psychodynamic*
- *Cognitive-Behavioral*
- *Humanistic/existential*

Each of these will be explained, as well as common variations. *It is important to keep in mind that degree and credentials have little bearing on what a psychotherapist's orientation will be.*

Each subsection, describing psychodynamic, cognitive-behavioral and humanistic/existential psychotherapy, will include a list of "buzz-names" and "buzz-words." These may be familiar to you or may be used by a prospective psychotherapist when discussing his or her theoretical orientation. They are provided so that when you hear them, you will be able to associate them with a particular orientation, and have a clearer idea of that psychotherapist's approach.

Psychodynamic theory and therapy

Freud was the first person to come up with an organized theory of the mind, taking ideas from biology, physics and philosophy. The theory he developed is called *psychoanalysis*. Since then, there have been numerous developments in psychoanalysis, and a more general term, *psychodynamic*, is used. There are four main subdivisions of psychodynamic theory and practice:

- Classical analysis
- Ego psychology
- Object relations
- Self psychology

Psychodynamic theories share some basic principles:

- The existence of an unconscious, preconscious and conscious (called the topographical model), and its importance in personality and behavior.
- The existence of the id, ego and superego (called the structural model).
- Conflict within different parts of the self is an inherent part of every human, and helps determine behavior, thoughts and feelings.
- The existence of transference, or the attribution of characteristics to another person that do not necessarily belong to that person, based on unconscious, unresolved conflict. Some say this exists in all human relationships whereas others focus on only the therapist/client relationship.
- The existence of resistance, or the natural human tendency to remain the same. (The exception to this is self-psychology, which will be discussed shortly.)
- Insight, or the reorganization of thoughts, feelings, and information, is necessary for an individual to make better choices for him/herself.

Classical analysis

Classical analysis, also referred to as psychoanalysis, refers to both a theory and practice of therapy. You may also hear the term psychoanalytic psychotherapy, which is based on the same concepts, but the patient will be face-to-face with the analyst (as opposed to on the couch), and the analyst will talk a bit more. Classical analysis is now more commonly practiced in this manner, with fewer analysts who will have you lay down on a couch and sit behind you.

It is a difficult task to describe classical analysis in a few pages, since there are hundreds and hundreds of books on this theory alone. But there are some "cornerstones" to the theory. Classical analysis involves "drives," explaining why it is often referred to as drive or instinct theory. The most basic of drives are what Freud called *eros* and *thanatos*, referring to the life (sex) and death (aggression) drives (Mishne, 1993). These drives are rooted in the unconscious and often problems arise because a person is resistant to acknowledging their power or even existence in his or her consciousness.

The id, ego and superego, located in the unconscious and conscious parts of the mind, are part of psychoanalytic theory as well. Here's a simple example to highlight the id, ego and superego and how they relate to one another. A ten-year-old boy is in a convenience store and has no money. He wants the candy bar he has been staring at. The part of his personality that says, "Take it, it'll taste good," is his id, based on the pleasure principle (or what one desires for satisfaction). This may be partly conscious and unconscious, meaning he is aware that he wants the candy bar, but unaware that the idea of stealing it is exciting to him. But then his superego kicks in and says, "It's wrong to steal." The superego is his value system. *This is a conflict, and it causes anxiety.* Then the executor of the mind, the ego says, "You will probably get caught, much like your friend did last week." The ego is based on the reality principle (or what one realistically expects). So, what will the kid do? If his ego and superego are in fact functioning properly, and the "energy" of his id is not out of control, he will not take the candy. The consequences for doing so would be possibly getting caught (ego), and feeling guilty (superego). While this simple example illustrates these concepts, people seek psychotherapy for more significant and complex reasons.

Another concept important to classical analysis is the presence of defense mechanisms, such as repression, regression, projection, denial and sublimation. Anna Freud (Sigmund's daughter) made a thorough study of the defense mechanisms and their importance to the person (she will be discussed in more detail in the ego psychology section). Finally, there are the psychosexual stages of development, including oral, anal, phallic, latent, and genital. You will see an alternative idea to these stages in the ego psychology section later on.

No discussion of psychoanalysis would be complete without mentioning some other theorists. So far, only concepts related to Freudian theory have been discussed. Two other important psychologists and contemporaries of Freud are Carl Jung and Alfred Adler. Carl Jung (pronounced "Yoong"), a well-educated and prolific analyst, developed a theory called analytical psychology that differed from Freudian theory. Analytical psychology does not limit the concept of "libido" to only sexual energy, but also includes drives such as creativity which strict Freudian theory does not. Also, Jung, after years of cross-cultural study, constructed the concept of a collective unconscious. This is found "below" (or deeper than) the personal unconscious, and involves "archetypes" or common symbols and experiences found in every human and culture he encountered. Some important concepts he introduced were "complex," "anima/animus," and "shadow" which originally belong to analytic psychology but now permeate our own culture and language.

The other person who deserves mention is Alfred Adler for his theory of individual psychology. Adler's focus is less on drives and more on the concept of self-determination. Individual psychology is concerned with an individual's striving, as an integrated whole, away from inferiority and towards superiority. Freud, Adler and Jung have had a tremendous impact on psychology all over the world, and play an influential role in psychology training, psychotherapy, and primary and secondary education.

What to expect from this type of psychotherapist

- This psychotherapist will listen more than he or she talks. (That is not to say that the therapist will not talk, but you will be doing more of it.)

- Generally, this approach is not a brief form of therapy and it will move at your pace.

- The therapist will ask questions that are intended to get you to organize information in a new way—helping you develop insight.

- You will find yourself talking about how the way you are *in* therapy applies to how you are *outside* of therapy. This will include thoughts, feelings and impressions that arise in the working relationship between you and the therapist.

- This therapist highly values the quality of the therapy relationship, since it is a reflection of other relationships in your life.

Buzz-names	S. Freud, Jung, Adler, Finechel, Rank, Ferenci, T. Reich
Buzz-words	Instinct, drive, id, ego, superego, unconscious, conscious, psychosexual stages (oral, anal, phallic, genital), defenses, Freudian slip (parapraxis, slip of the tongue), libido, cathexis, catharsis, transference, resistance, Oedipal conflict, free association, dream interpretation, transference

Ego psychology

Classical analysis envisions the id, based on the pleasure principle, to be the most powerful of the three forces in the mind (the other two being the ego and superego). Freud used the metaphor of a person on a horse, with the stronger, wilder, more primal horse representing the id, and the person with the reigns representing the ego. This meant that psychoanalysis was mostly a psychology of the unconscious. But even Freud, as his career went forward, began to give more attention and credence to the ego, which is after all, the "sense organ of the mind."

The "father of modern ego psychology," Heinz Hartmann, is dubbed as such because of his important assertion that there are conflict-free parts of the ego (Mishne, 1993). Hartmann discussed the ways in which the ego not only contributes to the defense mechanisms, but also mediates between the individual and the environment to help the individual adapt throughout life. With this development, such things as perception and motor development (ability to move around) were now attributed to the ego.

Anna Freud, who always envisioned herself carrying on her father's work, published her classic work, *The Ego and the Mechanisms of Defense*, in the late 1930's, creating a significant shift in psychodynamic thought. Far more attention was focused on the ego, and the defense mechanisms were considered as important, if not more important, than what that person may be defending against. For example, two professional basketball players both have strong aggressive impulses (rooted in the id). One player acts on these impulses by hurting other players and is regularly ejected from games. When interviewed about his harmful behavior, he responds that he is a "scapegoat," and is always being unfairly blamed for that which all players do because he is "flashy." This is one way of defending known as externalization. The other player uses these same aggressive impulses to intensely compete and dominate over other players, which is clear in his performance. The media views him as the "ultimate competitor" who plays with drive and will, rather than as an out-of-control menace. This is another way of defending known as sublimation. Both have the same drive, but the defenses each use to cope with that drive drastically change each player's behavior, feelings, thoughts, interactions and perception by others.

As mentioned earlier, the psychosexual stages are part of classical analysis. Erik Erikson, an ego psychologist, focused on identity as a central position in ego development (Mishne, 1993). This led to a very important shift, from the psycho*sexual* stages to the psycho*social* stages. One of the most significant differences between these two theories is that the psychosocial stages cover the lifespan, whereas the psychosexual stages only exist through adolescence. The psychosocial stages also focus on conflicts at each of eight stages of life, called the *stages of man*, most of which are more centered on social aspects of development and less on a sexual "zone."

What to expect from this type of psychotherapist

- This psychotherapist will listen more than he or she talks.
- Therapy will move at your pace and is traditionally not brief. (Brief forms do exist though.)
- There will be significant focus on how you handle both internal and external life-stressors.
- Focus will be on how your decisions benefit or hinder you.
- There will be an emphasis on your choices.
- This therapist highly values the quality of the therapist/client relationship since it is a reflection of other relationships in your life.

Buzz-names	Hartmann, A. Freud, E. Erikson, M. Mahler
Buzz-words	Defense mechanisms, adaptation, ego analysis, psychosocial stages, identity, separation-individuation, healthy symbiosis, rapprochement

Object relations

Object relations, although having much in common with classic analytic and ego psychology theory, is quite unique. First, it is important to note that "object" refers not to other persons but rather the internal representations of them; i.e. what that person represents. It views personality structure as developing in response to the individual's experiences with significant others, rather than heavily rooted in intrapsychic forces such as id and ego (Mishne, 1993).

Much of the study and focus in object relations is on how people relate to one another, and how each person's attitudes and behavior are affected by that relatedness (Mishne, 1993). John Bowlby, a skilled researcher and theorist in object relations, pioneered "attachment theory," focused on the early relationship between child and parent. Bowlby (1969) asserts, "What is believed to be essential for mental health is that the infant and young child should experience a warm, intimate and continuous relationship with his mother (or permanent mother-substitute) in which both find satisfaction and enjoyment. He further identified different types of attachment, and demonstrated the pathological impact of unhealthy attachment for adults later in life. Similarly, Winnicott termed "the holding environment" as an essential part of healthy infant and child development, in which mother provides a physical and emotional space in which the infant is protected without awareness (Mitchell & Black, 1995). This oblivious protection establishes an environment where the child can have "spontaneous experiences" that lead to healthy formation of self, since it is reliance on subjective experience through time that gives humans a sense of autonomous selfhood. Finally, Melanie Klein's theoretical writings discuss shifting "self/other configurations," or the internal images a person has for themselves and others, and accepted as instinct the infant's drive to attach.

What to expect from this type of psychotherapist
- This psychotherapist will listen more than he or she talks.
- This approach is generally not brief and will move at your pace. (Brief forms do exist though.)
- There will be more focus on your relationships, particularly how earlier relationships affect current relationships.
- You will discuss how your relationship with the therapist is similar to or different from others you have had.
- This therapist highly values the quality of the working relationship, since it is a reflection of other relationships in your life.

Buzz-names	Kernberg, M. Klein, Sullivan (most often considered his own classification), Hartmann (some consider him better classified here), Winnicott, Bowlby, Balint, Fairbairn
Buzz-words	Dynamism, healthy attachment, object, holding environment, good-enough mother, transitional object

Self psychology

Self psychology is the most recent psychodynamic approach, introduced solely by Heinz Kohut about twenty years ago. Empathy is a central concept in self psychology, as it also is in humanism (which will be discussed later). In fact, empathy in self psychology is eventually what "cures" the client. This is not a new idea to psychodynamic therapy, but self psychology emphasizes it much more than other forms of psychodynamic therapy. In fact, empathy is considered *necessary* in almost all psychology theories, but debate and disagreement arises when discussing whether or not empathy is *sufficient* for effective psychotherapy. Kohut (1975) has even gone so far as to say that psychoanalysis is the science of empathy, and because of this focus, self psychology has further closed the gap between theory and the practice of psychotherapy.

Self psychology differs greatly from classical analysis in many respects, one of them being that many functions attributed to the id, ego, and superego in classical analysis are attributed to the self in this theory. This approach is more holistic and treats the person as a whole—acting, feeling and thinking as a whole, rather than focusing on the conflicts between various parts.

What to expect from this type of psychotherapist

- This psychotherapist will talk a little more than other psychodynamic therapists, and the relationship will feel more "even".

- This approach is not a brief form of therapy, and it will move at your pace.

- There will be a great deal of focus on the therapy relationship.

• The relationship is central as it relates to the difficulties you are experiencing in life.

Buzz-names	Kohut
Buzz-words	Empathy (certainly not reserved for this approach), narcissistic personality disturbances, confirming responses, healthy narcissism

Cognitive-behavioral theory and therapy

John B. Watson coined the term *behaviorism*, and like many "isms", it has grown into a large and diverse branch of psychology. Behaviorism contends that it is only observable behavior that is valuable and that constructs such as mind, ego, self-actualizing tendency and self are impossible to measure or observe, and are therefore not amenable to change. But behaviorism, like all three forces in psychology, has proliferated and changed. Some of these changes have brought it closer to psychodynamic and humanistic thought, while others have sent it further away.

Along the way, behavioral theory became attached to cognitive theory, and the two have fused in many respects. Behaviorism refers to such principles as stimulus/response, classical and operant conditioning, punishment, reinforcement, modeling and so on. Cognitive theory deals with the way people think including intellect, and more importantly, thought processes. There are therapists, though, who consider themselves purely behavioral, and those who are much more focused on cognition rather than behavior. There are three main forms of cognitive-behavioral therapy:

- Behavior therapy
- Rational-emotive therapy
- Cognitive therapy

Cognitive-behavioral theories share some basic principles:
- Understanding the origins of a psychological problem is not essential for producing behavior change.
- Behavioral or cognitive-behavioral therapy involves a commitment to scientific method and empirically derived results.
- The "chicken or egg" argument of what comes first (the feeling or the thought) is unimportant because a therapist can intervene at any point.

- Abnormal behavior develops and is maintained by the same processes as normal behavior.

- Specific goals and objectives are essential and time limits are usually established.

Behavior therapy

Once, while both of us (Donna and Matt) were sitting in an IQ assessment class, our professor told us how he dealt with hyperactive children during IQ tests. He said, "You have to put them up on your lap, and when they respond, regardless if it's right or wrong, give them an M&M". This is an example, albeit simplified, of applying the behavioral technique of operant conditioning (i.e. increasing behaviors through reinforcement). In the example, rewarding the child's response with candy increases the frequency of responding. All animals, including humans, follow the principles of behaviorism. Whether we are determined to behave a certain way because of them, or whether they are the only principles at play is an area of much debate. Nevertheless, you may notice that cognitive-behavioral therapies are technique-driven, even though theorists and practitioners acknowledge the value of the working relationship.

Behavior therapy has had three major influences from which most behavioral techniques come. The first is applied behavior analysis, based on B.F. Skinner's (1953) "radical behaviorist" theory. *Radical behaviorism* asserts that nothing other than observable behaviors are relevant and will be the only thing dealt with in therapy. For instance, a radical behaviorist is more concerned with changing behavior than changing the thoughts or feelings associated with that behavior. From this perspective, the concepts of reinforcement, extinction, stimulus control and other procedures from laboratory research are applied. Applied behavior analysis generally does not use punishment unless safety is an issue, since it seems to suppress rather than eliminate unhealthy behavior so that the behavior likely returns when punishment is no longer present. So appropriate or beneficial behaviors will be verbally and otherwise reinforced, whereas harmful or "abnormal" behaviors will be ignored. The stimulus-response model, based on Pavlov and others' laboratory research is the second influence in behavior therapy. Stimulus-response techniques include systematic desensitization, flooding and in vivo exposure and have been effective for anxiety problems such as phobias. Finally, there is social learning theory that deals with concepts such as modeling (Bandura 1977). Modeling is the learning that occurs through observation. Generally, social learning theory considers thoughts and feelings private events and will not be directly addressed.

Nevertheless, behavior therapy will employ an integration of principles from applied behavior analysis, stimulus-response theory and social learning theory. Behavior therapy is used with children, adults, couples and groups.

What to expect from this type of psychotherapist

- This psychotherapist will talk as much if not more than you. (This probably will not be true until after the first few assessment sessions.)
- The work may feel more consultative or guidance-oriented.
- You will have specific tasks to practice both in and outside of the session.
- There can be record-keeping or journaling involved.
- You will likely spend more time talking about behaviors than thoughts and feelings.
- There will be specific techniques you will learn and take out of therapy.

Buzz-names	Skinner, Wolpe, Pavlov, Hull, Watson, Bandura
Buzz-words	Positive reinforcement, negative reinforcement, punishment, exposure, behavioral hierarchy, systematic desensitization, flooding, reciprocal inhibition, progressive relaxation, classical condition, operant conditioning, stimulus-response, modeling

Rational-emotive therapy (RET)

Rational-emotive therapy, or RET, is a form of cognitive-behavioral therapy based on the theory of the same name. It differs from other cognitive-behavioral approaches in that it accepts and values the role of feelings in its practice (Ellis, 1989). Albert Ellis, the theorist who "invented" RET, made an important contribution to behavioral theory in the 1950's. He holds that there is not a direct connection in people between a stimulus (or activating event—A), and a response (or emotional consequence—C). Rather, there is a belief system (B) in the middle that determines what the emotional consequence will be (Yankura & Dryden, 1990). Hence the A-B-C model was founded. The following is an example to illustrate. Your romantic partner just told you (s)he is breaking up with you. That is the stimulus or activating event (A). Strict behavioral thought would then predict a behavioral response or consequence (C), such as discomfort from not having the other person present anymore. But, according to RET, this is not the reason for the response. Rather a belief system (B) mediates the consequence (C). So if you believe that this means you will never find another partner, you will experience far more sadness or even depression. On the other hand, if you believe that (s)he is one of many persons who is capable of loving you, you will likely feel sadness from the loss, but much less so. The therapist comes in at point (D) and *actively* disputes irrational beliefs, such as, "I am unlovable." So this is an integrative model involving thoughts, feelings and behaviors.

What to expect from this type of psychotherapist

- This psychotherapist is highly active and will talk as much if not more than you.
- Tasks will be assigned to accomplish outside of therapy.
- Therapy will be brief.

- A "warm relationship" is not considered necessary, and you will be actively challenged regarding your thoughts and feelings that lead to unhealthy behaviors.
- Support, humor, role-playing and systematic desensitization may all be used.
- This therapy is focused on using logic to change.
- There will be specific goals and objectives to reach those goals.

Buzz-names	Ellis, Dryden
Buzz-words	Irrational belief, emotional consequence, belief system, RET

Cognitive therapy

Cognitive therapy is another theory and series of techniques that falls under the umbrella of cognitive-behavioral therapy. And although it is called cognitive therapy, with most of its influence on how people think, it too employs behavioral technique in addition to technique dealing with thought processes (Beck & Weishaar, 1989). The basic premise of Aaron T. Beck's cognitive therapy is that psychological problems such as anxiety disorders, depressive disorders, obsessive-compulsive disorder, etc., exist because of a person's biases in processing information. In other words, psychological difficulties may result for an individual who develops certain ways of thinking about events, the future and him/herself that are unhealthy. These unhealthy ways of thinking, called "schemas" or templates develop through life experiences and are activated by stress. Using the RET example of a romantic break-up, if you selectively attend to themes of loss or defeat after your break-up, you will likely experience depression. Certainly an amount of grief and sadness is considered "normal" from this perspective. But cognitive therapy contends that specific attitudes predispose people to interpret events in a biased manner (Beck & Weishaar, 1989).

One way cognitive therapy differs from RET is in treatment strategy. In this therapy there is a collaborative approach, in which both therapist and patient together can weed out dysfunctional biases and then change them. Another stylistic difference is using "guided discovery," or finding the pathways from the person's past that have led to misperceptions and misinterpretations. In this way, cognitive therapy is not unlike psychodynamic theory and practice. In fact, Beck acknowledges influence from psychodynamic thought as well as the phenomenological approach that we will discuss in the humanistic/existential section.

The techniques in cognitive therapy are used to help the patient shift his or her thoughts in a manner that is more adaptive and functional. Beliefs are explored and tested as hypotheses for how adaptive or "accurate" they actually are. Some of the cognitive distortions Beck (1972) points out during psychological distress include *overgeneralization* or "Nobody likes me," after being rejected by one person, and *dichotomous thinking* which most people know as "black and white thinking". Cognitive therapy is not only techniques but also a set of models for anxiety, depression and phobias. The therapy is highly structured and short-term, usually lasting no more than sixteen weeks. Finally, this therapy, much like RET and behavior therapy, is a problem-oriented approach meant to address specific difficulties and is not designed for personal growth (Beck & Weishaar, 1989).

What to expect from this type of psychotherapist

- This psychotherapist will be active and will ask many questions (Socratic questioning) as he or she explores hypotheses with you, especially after the first few sessions.

- Tasks will be assigned to accomplish outside of therapy.

- Therapy will be brief and highly structured.

- The basic qualities of empathy, acceptance and personal regard are valued by the therapist.

- Systematic desensitization and other behavioral techniques may be used.

- This therapy is also highly focused on logic.

- There will be specific goals and tasks to reach those goals.

Buzz-names	Beck, Lazarus, Mahoney, Meichenbaum
Buzz-words	Cognitive distortion, "black and white thinking," cognitive restructuring, overgeneralization, personalization, guided discovery, systematic desensitization

Humanistic/existential theory and therapy

Humanistic/existential theory and practice represents, once again, a major break from the psychological thought that preceded it. It is considered the "third force" because of the weight it has carried within the field along with psychodynamic and cognitive-behavioral theories and therapies. It is grounded in phenomenological and existential philosophy, and therefore differs significantly from psychodynamic and behavioral theory and psychotherapy. So what is phenomenology? It refers to the *phenomenal realm* or purely subjective experience. Phenomenology maintains that the only way for a science of psychology to understand anything is to see it from a person's own or *subjective* point of view (Rychlak, 1981). Even more simply put, reality is perception, and there is no ultimate reality. We all perceive only what our senses allow us to see which is our personal reality. Consequently, mind and body cannot be separated, and both forms of experience are united in the conception of a person's *phenomenal field*. An easy way to think about this is that each person is a world or a universe unto him or herself. That person's thoughts, feelings and experiences are unique, based not only on his or her genetic makeup and social, cultural, and familial influences, but also on characteristics that are completely unique to the individual.

Existential theory, while sharing much with phenomenological thought, is interested in profound questions about the human being, such as the nature of despair, loneliness, anxiety and isolation. Yet it is still primarily concerned with the phenomenological world in which a person exists and participates.

Both existential psychology and humanistic psychology stem from a deep concern that science is attempting to reduce the human being to only the observable, and that much is lost when this occurs. Carl Jung, a psychoanalyst from whom much has been taken in forming humanistic and existential thought, makes an exceptionally insightful and important point regarding the traditional scientific approach to psychology. He makes the point that one could gather a hundred stones and weigh them collectively. The total weight might be 100 pounds. Then, one could calculate the average weight of each stone, which would of course equal one pound per stone. But you could take each and every stone, weigh it individually, and never find one that weighs one pound. The point being made by the phenomenological stance is that psychology is a science of individuals, and techniques based on the data of averages could potentially apply to no one. As such, practitioners should approach each person from an individual perspective instead of from a set of techniques or preconceived theories about human nature. The idea is to develop the "theory" from the person sitting with the therapist based on who that person is and where (s)he comes from, rather than apply a previously constructed theory to each person. The three main theories subsumed under humanistic/existential theory and therapy are:

- Client-centered therapy
- Existential therapy
- Gestalt therapy

Humanistic-existential theories share some basic principles:

- People's creative power is a crucial force in their lives, in addition to heredity and environment.
- Persons are integrated wholes and are best treated that way, as opposed to treating pieces of the person such as one's thoughts or behaviors.
- Humans are best understood by appreciating the individual's subjectivity (phenomenology), including thoughts, feelings, senses, intuitions and nonconscious.
- Traditional scientific method is limiting in the understanding of individuals and human nature because it views itself as objective and is concerned more with what is observable.
- Psychotherapy is essentially based on a good human relationship between client and therapist.

(*Some of these are taken from Ansbacher, 1977, p.51—Current Therapies, p. 158)

Client-centered therapy

Client-centered therapy is the most significant theory and therapy within humanistic psychology, with principles like genuineness, warmth, empathy, and positive regard that are considered basic to all therapies. Humanism considers these factors necessary and sufficient for positive change and growth, whereas other theories view them as only the foundation.

Client-centered therapy is named as such because it suggests that the "client is in the driver's seat." In other words, the client sets the agenda, pace, and direction of therapy. Originally, Carl Rogers (the originator and researcher of this theory and approach) referred to it as nondirective therapy, but spent most of his career trying to retract that label because it suggested there was no direction at all. His intention was to make it clear that the therapist was not going to direct the client, which is commonplace in cognitive-behavioral approaches. You may notice that it has much in common with the psychodynamic version of self-psychology.

Concepts specific to client-centered therapy include the following:
- Certain attitudes (empathy, positive regard, genuineness) in therapists constitute the *necessary and sufficient* conditions for therapy effectiveness.
- Therapists need to be immediately present and accessible to clients, relying on their moment-to-moment experiencing in the relationships.
- There is continual and intense focus on the subjective world of the client.
- Positive change in therapy is marked by a shift in the client towards living more in the present.
- There is a concern with the process of change rather than personality structure.
- There is value in the need for continued research to learn more about psychotherapy.
- The same principles apply to all persons regardless of diagnosis; i.e. psychotic, bipolar, etc.
- Psychotherapy is one special example of a healthy relationship.

- The psychotherapist's determination is to create a theory out of being with the person, rather than forcing the person to fit a preformed theory.

- There is a concern for the philosophical issues related to the practice of psychotherapy.

(Rogers & Sanford, 1985)

Client-centered therapy believes in the natural and organismic tendency to strive towards one's fullest potential, or *the self-actualizing tendency* (Raskin & Rogers, 1989). You may have heard the term *self-actualization*, which comes from humanistic philosophy and psychology.

What to expect from this type of psychotherapist

- This psychotherapist values "being with you in the moment" above all else, as well as allowing his or her empathy, genuineness and positive regard to show.

- Directives will not be given and you will lead where the therapy goes.

- There will be a deep respect for you as a whole, including those aspects of yourself that you like and those you dislike.

- The focus will be on the "here-and-now," or what you are experiencing as you sit in therapy. (Note-psychodynamic approaches also may have this quality.)

- There will be a focus on what your personal reality is, and how you subjectively experience life.

Buzz-names	Rogers, Maslow, Bugental, Ansbacher, Charkoff, Truax, Axline (child play therapy), Gendlin, Raskin
Buzz-words	Validation, congruence, empathy, unconditional positive regard, locus-of-evaluation, self-concept, self-worth, self-actualization, actualizing tendency, internal frame of reference, reflection (the technique, not the act)

Existential therapy

Existential therapy is primarily concerned with understanding the client as he or she exists in his/her world, hence the prefix "exist" in the term "existential." The "world" referred to is the same as the phenomenal field in humanism. Therefore, existential therapy is derived from an integration of phenomenological and existential philosophies. There are a few different existential approaches to therapy, most developed independently in different parts of Europe. Most of what we will discuss is derived from Rollo May's existential therapy.

From the existential perspective, the individual is not a machine or even a complex machine, but rather an emerging being. This emerging is closely tied to that individual's sense of meaning (Patterson, 1973; May & Yalom, 1989), and is evident in the therapy because the psychotherapist will often ask in a variety of ways, "What does that mean for [to] you?" None of the existential therapies present a systematic approach, like the cognitive-behavioral therapies, and there is little focus on techniques. Similar to client-centered therapy, existential psychotherapy is a way of being, and not a way of doing for the therapist. There are many concepts unique to existentialism. This therapy is more closely tied to philosophy than any other, but you need not be philosophically-minded to benefit.

Some concepts particularly valued by existentialism are:

- Humans are distinct in that we are aware of ourselves and our existence, as well as our past, present and future. This means that choice and decision are possible (free-will). This then means that we are responsible because we can choose. Humans are therefore free, and we are what we make of ourselves. Factors such as heredity, environment and society have an impact, but they only limit, rather than determine, our choices.

- The person and his/her world are inseparable. Each human lives in three worlds simultaneously; that of the biological world, the "being-in-self" or self-identity world, and the world of others and environment. Individuals are not static and each evolves and emerges to create *being*.

- The human knows he or she will eventually die; thus the meaning of existence implies nonexistence. This must be confronted, because it is death that gives life meaning. This is a natural and normal source of anxiety, often called existential anxiety or "angst."

- Each person has inherent uniqueness apart from cultural/familial influences.

- The human is increasingly alienated from the world and community as societies "advance," which creates problems in living; i.e. detachment, isolation, etc. (Patterson, 1973)

Existential therapy deals with the person as he/she exists in the world at the moment with all accompanying anxiety and guilt, both of which can be considered either "normal" or unhealthy. Therapy will be focused on the two persons in the room, one being a person who is a psychotherapist and one who is not. Concepts such as the unfairness of life, unavoidable death, acceptance of ultimate aloneness (that we must ultimately make our own choices), and acknowledging responsibility for who we are and our choices are all key beliefs to existential therapy and philosophy.

What to expect from this type of psychotherapist

- This psychotherapist will value "being with you in the moment" and will be comfortable letting his or her genuine identity show.

- This therapist believes in the importance of you being exceptionally aware of your existence and its personal meaning for you.

- There will be an expectation that you are ultimately responsible for who you are, with the understanding that circumstances and childhood experiences have significant impact.

- This therapist will show a deep respect for you as you exist in your three worlds (see above).
- Focus will be on the "here-and-now," and how you are emerging as your life continues.
- Focus will be on what your personal reality is, and how you subjectively experience.

Buzz-names	R. May, Binswanger, Boss, Frankl, Sartre
Buzz-words	Existential angst, existential anxiety, death anxiety, logotherapy, free-will

Gestalt therapy

Gestalt therapy, also a phenomenological-existential therapy based on the like philosophies, is focused on present awareness, rather than interpreting and reflecting. Fritz and Laura Perls, who were husband and wife, founded and wrote prolifically about gestalt therapy. In this therapy, the process (or what is going on in the session between therapist and client) is much more important than the content (or what is being said). Once again, similar to client-centered and existential therapies, it maintains an emphasis on the person as a whole in his/her environment. In this regard, mind, body and spirit cannot be teased apart and the healthy person is a complete thinking, feeling and behaving being (Yontef & Simkin, 1989).

Gestalt therapy takes many ideas from classical Freudian psychoanalytic theory, such as instincts and a striving for balance. But it diverges in more respects than it follows. This is particularly true in its use of techniques such as role-playing and "empty chair technique," in which a client imagines talking to a particular person in his or her life in the empty chair. Gestalt therapy uses heightened awareness and experimentation to move towards insight (Yontef & Simkin, 1989). However, how the therapist and client experience their relationship is the most important aspect of the therapy.

The therapeutic relationship, founded on "existential dialogue," grows out of contact between "me" and "not-me" (Yontef & Simkin, 1989).

Some concepts particularly important to the gestalt perspective are:
- There is no reality other than the present, so the "here-and-now" is key.
- Most people are lacking in awareness of their functioning as a whole person and organism.
- Problems are caused by avoiding awareness of self.
- Awareness requires heightened concentration, and various techniques are used to further concentration and awareness.
- "Digging" for the root of problems is unnecessary if awareness of what is obvious is brought in the open.
- The therapist allows him or herself to be in the interpersonal process. It is not manipulated or controlled in any way.
- "What is, is." Awareness of this alone leads to spontaneous change. (Yontef & Simkin, 1989)

Gestalt therapy encourages experiencing and thought related to that experience, rather than reflecting or distancing from experiences. Its techniques are unique and innovative, setting it apart from client-centered and existential therapy where there is little emphasis on techniques. Cognitive-behavioral therapies, although involving many techniques, use far fewer experiential techniques than gestalt therapy.

What to expect from this type of psychotherapist
- The focus will be on a genuine person-to-person relationship between you and the therapist.
- There will be encouragement of increasing awareness of you as a whole person, employing various techniques or exercises to do this.

- This therapist will be ready and willing to challenge your way of being and how it hinders awareness, thereby causing problems in living.
- There will be a real interpersonal dialogue in which the therapist will at times share his/her subjective (phenomenological) perspective or express feelings when appropriate.
- There will be a focus on the "here-and-now" and how you are emerging as your life continues.
- There will be a focus on what your personal reality is, and how you subjectively experience yourself, others, and your world.
- You will be encouraged to build your own supports (ability to make contact or withdraw from others).

Buzz-names	F. Perls, L. Perls, Simkin, Yontef
Buzz-words	Existential dialogue, here-and-now, "me/not-me," empty chair technique, experiential, I-thou relation, guided fantasy, enactment

Conclusion

The major theoretical orientations and more specific therapies that come out of each have been discussed in this chapter. The following graph illustrates these for you. Most research that has compared these various therapies has shown that they are generally equally effective, although there are some differences depending on the problem you are bringing to therapy.

THE 3 SCHOOLS

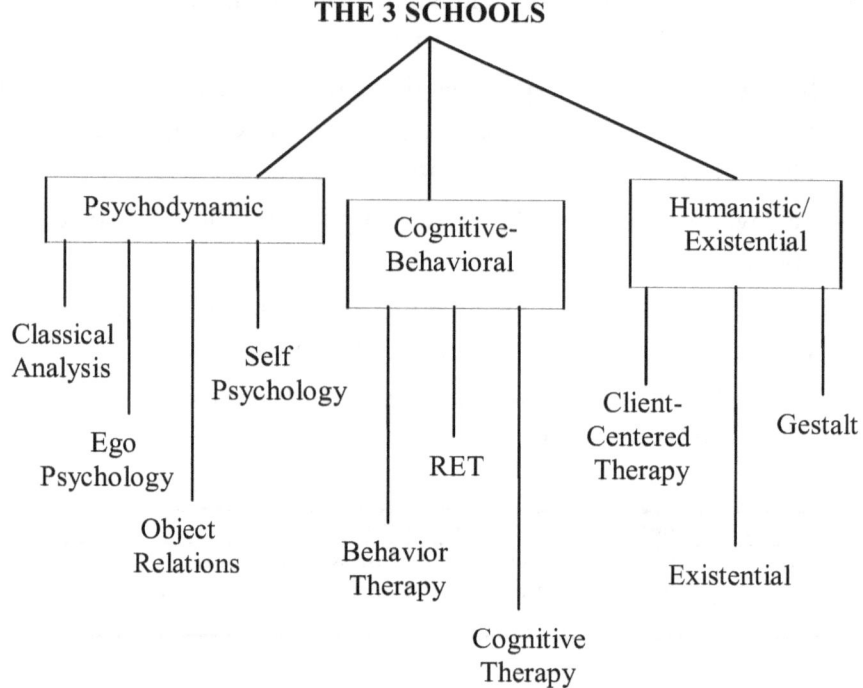

CHAPTER 5: TYPES OF PSYCHOTHERAPY

You may now have a better understanding of how different therapists envision helping individuals. That was the first of the three pillars of psychotherapy that are helpful in identifying an appropriate therapist. In this chapter the second pillar, type of psychotherapy, is discussed.

Psychotherapists not only come from particular theoretical orientations, but they apply these orientations to different types of therapy. The term "types" refers to individual, group, couples, family or child psychotherapy. The particular theoretical orientation does not necessitate a specific type of therapy that a psychotherapist practices. For instance, you will be able to find cognitive-behavioral individual therapists, cognitive-behavioral family therapists, and cognitive-behavioral child therapists. Similarly, you will find psychodynamically oriented child therapists, as well as humanistic child therapists. Of course the type of therapy mandates differences within the approach. It would be ridiculous if a psychotherapist, regardless of orientation, spoke to an adult the same way as a child.

Also in this chapter, you are given useful information regarding brief therapy since most psychotherapy today is time-limited. Finally, psychological testing is explained. Although this is not "psychotherapy," we thought it would be useful to you, since testing and psychotherapy sometimes go hand-in-hand.

Furthermore, consequent to increasing specialization in the massive field of psychotherapy, more specialized theories and practices have been put forth, most of which are derived from one of the three major orientations discussed in the last chapter. For example, Virginia Axline's play therapy for children is considered humanistic or client-centered, whereas Melanie Klein's play therapy is derived from a more psychodynamic basis. In this chapter these types are explained, so that you can pursue a particular *type of therapy* as your primary goal if you so choose, with *theoretical orientation* being secondary to you.

Individual therapy

The theoretical orientation chapter (Chapter 4) discusses the major types of therapy for individuals. So to spare you redundancy, it will not be discussed again in this chapter.

Group therapy

Historically, group therapy was thought of as a back-up, or "second-rate" therapy, to be used when individual therapy did not seem to be going particularly well. This attitude still lingers for some practitioners and mental health facilities. That is very unfortunate. Group therapy can in fact often be the treatment of choice for particular problems. Furthermore, group therapy in conjunction with individual therapy is a powerful combination for many problems including, but certainly not limited to:

- Eating difficulties and body image concerns
- Survivors of trauma
- Difficulties with anger and acting out towards others
- Self-esteem issues
- Discomfort relating to others
- Patterns of unsuccessful relationships
- Fear of social situations
- Depression
- General anxiety

This is only a brief list, and there are many other excellent topics in which group therapy is highly effective. It is natural for you to feel less comfortable sharing personal problems with a group of people as compared to a single therapist. In fact, most people feel that way. But group therapy can be more effective to you for that very reason, and one of the most common experiences for an individual in a group is the realization that others feel similarly and struggle with similar issues. Furthermore, group therapy is usually less expensive than individual therapy.

There are, as with other types of therapy, psychodynamically-oriented, behavioral and client-centered groups (Shaffer & Galinsky, 1989). But group therapy has its own theory as well. Group or interpersonal dynamics are different from dynamics between two people, and from the dynamics and conflicts experienced internally or "intrapsychically." Irvin Yalom's (1985) *Theory and Practice of Group Psychotherapy* is considered the most comprehensive book addressing the tremendous amount of research and theory on group psychotherapy. Yalom himself has an existential orientation, but his group work is somewhat independent of that. The types of groups stemming from this work are called process groups, because in addition to dealing with the subjects discussed in the group, the ways in which members relate to each other and the therapist are explored. Some issues important to group theory and psychotherapy are universality (commonality of certain problems and feelings), altruism, development of socializing techniques, corrective emotional experiences, insight, and recognition of problematic behavioral patterns, to name only a few (Yalom, 1985). Process groups can be time-limited or unlimited, open or closed to new members, and homogenous or heterogeneous (different problems among members). By definition, the group leader of a process group does not direct the content, and there is no specific topic. In addition, you will have no difficulty finding psychodynamic, existential-experiential, psychodrama or gestalt groups if you are interested. Many of these groups are exclusively for women, men, or mixed gender.

The other major class of group therapy is those that are topic-driven. For instance, groups could be offered for those who suffer from panic attacks. Often, such groups have a psychoeducational component, in which the leader imparts information for part of the group and then discussion takes place. These groups are almost always time-limited, and the number of weeks is established before you join. Each week usually has certain topics to discuss. You may notice that this seems to be a closer derivative of behavior theory. This is in part true in that the sessions are more structured and didactic (teaching-like), but the group will not necessarily be focused on behaviors only.

Topic-driven groups are generally better if you have a specific request such as a phobia or difficulty relaxing, whereas process groups are better for self-understanding and personal growth.

Groups can be found for both adults and children. Groups for children will understandably be more topic-driven, depending on the age range in the group, since kids are not particularly strong in the ways of self-reflection. Groups for attention deficit disorder (with or without hyperactivity), school refusal, and various behavioral problems are common for children.

For almost all psychotherapy groups, regardless of what type it is, the group or co-leaders will want to interview you before a decision is made as to whether or not group is best for you. This serves multiple purposes, including allowing you to assess your comfort with the leader, for you to determine if the group topic and others in the group will work for your needs, and for the leader to make similar assessments.

There are also many self-help groups in most communities. Alcoholics Anonymous (AA), Narcotics Anonymous (NA) and Over-eaters Anonymous (OA) are examples of 12-step groups, and locations can be found by calling your state's mental health association or the 12-step numbers listed in the "Resources" chapter of this book. In addition, there are many non-12-step groups, including men's and women's groups. Keep in mind that a self-help group is *not* psychotherapy, will most often not have a therapist or counselor present, and is focused on support and advice.

Most often, psychotherapists who do group therapy do not do so exclusively. So do not expect to find a therapist who tells you that is all s(he) does. Furthermore, if you are interested in a process group, you will want someone who has experience running that type of group, and it is less important that the therapist have significant experience with the specific problem(s) you are bringing to the group.

Remember that in a process group, it is the group that will do more of the helping than the leader, and it is the leader's role to facilitate the formation of the group into a helping body. On the other hand, if you are pursuing a topic-driven group in which the therapist will be doing psychoeducation, it is more important for that psychotherapist to have experience with the particular problem you wish to work on.

Child therapy

Children lack the ability to effectively put their feelings into words. As children mature, they become better at this. But the younger the child, the more difficulty s(he) will have expressing how s(he) feels. That is why when children are sad, scared or angry, they are more likely to say they have a "tummy ache," or even more simply, "I feel bad," rather than "I am feeling sad and alone." The child may in fact be physically sick, and a medical doctor should always check that out first if complaints are common. But if you determine as a parent that there are emotional or behavioral problems, then psychotherapy may be appropriate. So how does a psychotherapist work with a child, since most of what we have discussed thus far has been about talk therapies? Enter play therapy and behavior therapy. Keep in mind that family therapy and cognitive approaches are also used, but play and behavior therapy are the most common individual child therapies.

Play therapy

Play therapy is just what it sounds like. It is a form of therapy that uses play with the child to assess and treat problems the child is experiencing at home, school or in the community. The psychotherapist, who will be a specialist in child and adolescent psychotherapy, will determine whether the child will benefit more from play therapy or talk therapy. Most of this decision will be based on the maturity level of the child, taking into account age, awareness of feelings, and how verbal the child or adolescent is. Another clue is if, when the therapist tries to "analyze" the child, he/she tells the therapist, "I'm bored," or "You're boring," and goes back to the toys. The two most significant types of play therapy are psychodynamic play therapy, based on the theory and practice of Melanie Klein or Anna Freud (Sigmund's daughter), and client-centered or humanistic play therapy, based on Virginia Axline's work.

Melanie Klein believed that child's play was the equivalent of free association for adults (Tuma & Russ, 1993). Her method, which is commonly employed, involves continual interpretation of the child's play and behavior. Her theory is usually referred to as the English school of child psychoanalysis, so if you hear that phrase, that is where it comes from. Her theory has had lasting impact on both work with children and object relations theory applied to adults. Anna Freud's psychodynamic method involves more conservative interpretation of play and behavior, theorized to be a reflection of internal conflicts (also true in Kleinian theory). A. Freud also suggested treatment for a far more restricted range of children, whereas Klein viewed "neuroses" as part of being a child and coping with natural child development (Tuma & Russ, 1993). A. Freud's technique is much more focused on a child's tendency to deny problems and resist attempts at treatment. The relationship is therefore very close, much closer than it would be with an adult in classic psychoanalysis, and it is essential for the child to want to come to sessions. A. Freud's theory and practice is often referred to as the American school of child psychoanalysis, since it blossomed in the

United States. This occurred in spite of the fact that her Vienna Center was closed down by the Nazi's in 1938, at which time she moved to London and set up a wartime center for infants and children.

Virginia Axline, the major theorist in client-centered child therapy, was a student of Carl Rogers (the founder of client-centered therapy) at Ohio State University. In her classic book, *Play therapy*, Axline (1947) outlines eight basic principles of "non-directive play therapy," which either add to or duplicate concepts put forth by Rogers. These include:

- An emphasis on warmth and friendliness
- Unconditional acceptance of the child
- A feeling of permissiveness so the child can express freely
- An alertness to the feelings of the child
- A deep respect for the child's ability to solve his/her own problems
- Allowing the child to direct his/her own actions and conversation
- Allowing the child to move at his/her natural pace
- Establishing limitations only to anchor therapy and make the child aware of his/her responsibility in the relationship

(Axline, 1947)

There is no interpretation in this type of play therapy (as in psychodynamic play therapy), but rather reflection. In this way, the child's natural potential can emerge as opposed to having something done to the child.

Child behavior therapy

Behavior therapy employs the same principles to children as it does to adults, such that putting feelings into words is not essential. Talk is important in behavior therapy to communicate various techniques, discuss how they are going and how to modify them, and discuss problematic factors that maintain "unhealthy behaviors" and do not allow the practice of new, more adaptive ones. A parent can closely monitor these behaviors.

Techniques such as changing reinforcement schedules, increasing positive reinforcement for acceptable behaviors and reducing inappropriate behaviors through limit-setting are common for behavior problems, but specific sets of techniques depend on the problem. For instance, if the child is school phobic, a technique called in vivo (real) exposure may be employed. In all cases, consistency is essential. The child behavior therapist will therefore want close contact with parents, teachers, coaches, and maybe even siblings if they are old enough to contribute to treatment.

Couples therapy

Many people now go to couples therapy. For a long time and until recently, couples therapy was called "marital therapy." There are two problems with this. First, gay and lesbian couples cannot legally be married in most states. Thus, many gay and lesbian persons were not engaging in marital therapy, in spite of relationship problems, because the theoretical underpinnings and political atmosphere suggested that homosexual couples were unwelcome. Second, social norms have changed drastically in the past forty years, and many couples now live together (co-habitate) before or instead of marriage. It is more and more common for heterosexual unmarried couples to attend couples therapy. Previously, many were "turned off" by the term "marital therapy" which can be threatening to those who have not chosen to marry. The term "marital therapy" led to confusion and questions like, "Can we go if we are not married," or "Will the therapy be focused on moving us toward marriage?" The answer to the first is obviously "Yes," and the answer to the second is "No," with the exception of some types of pastoral counseling. But in the last twenty years, those in the mental health field have recognized these problems and have very quickly worked toward creating solutions. So, it is now termed couples therapy.

There are four major theoretical models of couples therapy: *psychoanalytic, social-learning-cognitive, structural-strategic,* and *systems model* (Jacobson & Gurman, 1986). We know we said we were done with theoretical orientation, but we do promise that we will discuss theory only as it applies to the specific application of couples therapy.

Psychoanalytic model of couples therapy

Psychoanalytic couples therapy is rooted in psychodynamic thought and would be more accurately named psychodynamic couples therapy. This approach is insight-oriented and will be focused on helping the couple gain an understanding of the nature of the relationship, as well as the problems that trouble them within that relationship (Dare, 1986).

Social-learning-cognitive model of couples therapy

The social-learning-cognitive perspective is rooted in behavioral theory (Jacobson & Holtzworth-Munroe, 1986). However, more complex theories and practices for couples therapy grew out of behavioral theory, because treating couples is more complicated than treating individuals and because controlled-outcome research in behavioral marital therapy showed that standard behavioral techniques are not always effective in couples work (Jacobson & Holtzworth-Munroe, 1986). From this perspective, there certainly will be a focus on behaviors and a common goal may be to increase the ratio of positive to negative behavior exchanges (a common problem in distressed relationships). Also, much focus will be on building skills, such as conflict resolution, in order to maintain an intimate relationship over time. Finally, reinforcement erosion will be addressed. This is the tendency for partners in a relationship to slowly cease giving each other psychological "goodies" over time.

Structural-strategic model of couples therapy

The structural-strategic model of couples therapy is an integration of two traditionally opposing stances, one being the structural model, and the other being the strategic model (what a surprise). But both share some assumptions, such as the importance of the current context as opposed to history. Additionally, the structural-strategic model takes a life-cycle view in which symptoms are viewed in that developmental context, and believed to be caused by the relationship, rather than by either of the individuals (Todd, 1986). From this perspective, the behavior in the partnership is seen as guided by each of the partners individually, the feedback between them, and the impact of outside sources such as children, other family, occupational factors, friends, etc. The therapist will be active and directive in order to get the couple to find new ways to behave toward one another.

Systems model of couples therapy

Systems theory is in many ways similar to the structural-strategic model. There are various forms of systems theory, which is the final major approach to couples therapy discussed. The most widely used is Bowen's (1978) family systems model. From this perspective, partner conflict comes from the interactive influences in the self-system, extended-family system (families of origin), and the couple-nuclear family system (Bowen, 1978). Developmental and personality factors play into the self-system, and all of that interacts with a number of factors in the two other systems. This theoretical approach is also very common in family therapy. One of the most interesting things about this approach is the development of a charting method to better illustrate quality and closeness of relatedness between people. A member of the couple will come to understand, without feeling a sense of blame, the many influences that affect his or her behavior in the current relationship.

Family therapy

There are four major schools of family therapy, three of which are humanistic, psychodynamic, and behavioral family therapy. The fourth and most significant approach to family therapy is systemic family therapy, and its many variations (Hansen & L'Abate, 1982). Systems psychology has not been thoroughly discussed yet because it is generally applied to family therapy, or sometimes couples therapy as mentioned earlier. But it is now the major force in family therapy and a therapist can be specially trained in that theoretical group of therapies. Those trained and credentialed in marriage and family therapy will have such specialized knowledge and training.

Psychodynamic and humanistic models of family therapy

Ackerman's psychodynamically influenced family therapy addresses the need for the family to shift the balance of roles (Hanson & L'Abate, 1982). This occurs by learning to relate to each other in new ways. Ackerman makes no clear distinction between "healthy" and "sick" families, but viewed families with problems as those that fail to carry out essential family functions. Virginia Satir's family therapy has been influenced by experiential, gestalt, existential and client-centered thought. Her theory is truly eclectic, with systems psychology rooting the many influences. This theory maintains the importance of becoming aware that the identified patient is a reflection of patterns of family interaction (Satir, 1971). For example, a person struggling with anorexia nervosa may be reflecting issues of control, communication, and expression of the anger in the family. Furthermore, similar to humanistic/existential thought, Satir's family therapy holds as an assumption that "sickness" is a communication of reaching out for help, and that humans naturally strive towards their full potential (Hansen & L'Abate, 1982).

Systems models of family therapy

Haley, a "communications analyst" who formed strategic therapy, discovered common effective factors in psychotherapy while devising his approach. The theory stresses the family as a system in which actions and reactions of one member influence actions and reactions of other members (Hanson & L'Abate, 1982). The approach involves the therapist giving directives to family members. It emphasizes the whole family engaging in such exercises. The intent is to change the family's complex, dysfunctional and rigid ways of interacting so all members will benefit. Strategic therapy can also be used for individual or couples but is most often applied to family therapy.

The paradox and counterparadox model comes out of the Milan Group from Italy. This was a group of four Italian physicians originally trained in psychoanalysis who formed the Milan Center for Family Studies. The theory finds its basis in systems psychology, human communication and cybernetics (which will not be discussed here) (Hansen & L'Abate, 1982). Some assumptions of the approach suggest that it is impossible not to communicate, and that every behavior takes place on both a content level (verbal) and a nonverbal level. The ultimate goal of this therapy is to transform the family system so it is less rigid. The therapist will be active and positive but will take a neutral, participant role.

Minuchin's structural theory of family therapy, also a systems approach, focuses on changing the organization of the family so that members and the family as a whole functions more adaptively. The theory holds that adaptation in a family occurs as the result of inner pressure (the result of developmental changes in the family), and outer pressure either from others or environmental changes (Hanson & L'Abate, 1982). The family structure is a set of functional demands that organizes how family members will behave. Global themes can be found from these demands and then changed, largely because the therapist becomes part of the new social system and works to guide from within.

Bowen's system theory represents a unique form of systems psychology as well. As discussed in the couples therapy section, "illness" is viewed as a relationship between people, and therefore change in one person will inevitably create a change in anyone else involved in a relationship with that person (Bowen, 1978). A genogram, or a type of family tree, will be created, which includes the nature of relationships between family members. The following is an example of a genogram used by many family therapists. The genogram is created collaboratively by the therapist and family in the assessment or beginning phase of family therapy.

SAMPLE GENOGRAM

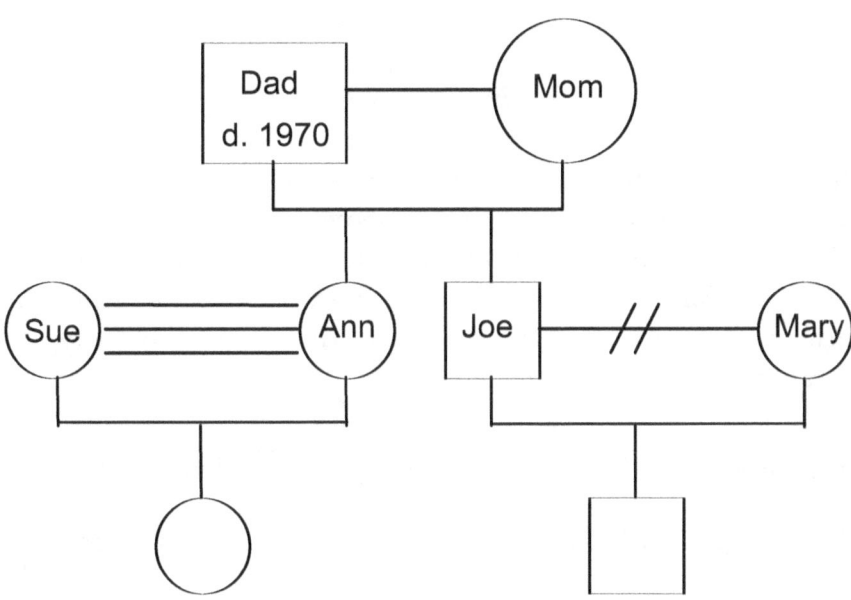

In this example of a genogram, various family relationships are depicted (squares represent males and circles represent females). Mom and Dad (who died in 1970) have two children—Ann and Joe. Ann is involved in a lesbian relationship with Sue, and is overly attached to her, as depicted by the three lines. They have one daughter. Joe and Mary are divorced with one son. The divorce is denoted by slashes through the connecting line. This is just one simplified example of a genogram that some therapists (family therapists, in particular) may use to help them keep track of a client's many relationships.

The goal of treatment is for family members to become more individualized while still remaining connected. As one member becomes more individualized, changes occur in all of the many relationships within the family system, so guidance, support and encouragement are necessary.

There are, as with all types of therapy, many more forms of family therapy. But these are the ones that you will most commonly encounter when you ask the proper questions of a family therapist.

Brief therapy

In these days of managed care, where the credo is often efficiency, brief therapy is increasingly common. In fact, more therapy being done today is brief (or short-term) rather than open-ended. Brief therapists come from most orientations, including psychodynamic, cognitive-behavioral, and humanistic/existential. The following chart will help simplify the type and orientation issue:

Dynamic	Individual*	Couples*	Group*	Family*	Child
Cognitive-Behavioral	Individual*	Couples*	Group*	Family*	Child
Humanistic	Individual*	Couples*	Group*	Family*	Child

Can be done in brief form of therapy

This chart is not entirely accurate because it does not discuss the many variants of each major theoretical orientation. For instance, classic psychoanalysis is not a brief form of therapy in the United States, and persons engaged in this therapy attend sessions at least twice a week for a period of years. But we thought it could be helpful to simply visualize what can seem perplexing. You can see that brief therapy can be done with most therapies. *This does not mean that it is usually done in most therapies, only that it can be.*

Cognitive-behavioral therapy has traditionally been brief, lasting somewhere from 10-20 sessions, whereas psychodynamic therapy has only developed briefer models in the past few decades. Humanistic theory and practice still struggles with theoretical differences between it and limited therapy, although interesting forms are being created like accelerated empathy therapy. You also may have noticed that child therapy is generally not done in brief form. The reason for this is that it usually takes more time to form a therapeutic relationship with a child so that effective work can be done. However, this does not rule out a shorter-term therapy with a particular child, if that child bonds more quickly to the psychotherapist and presents with a limited problem.

If you are interested in brief therapy, or are feeling limited by your insurance, then you will want to ask questions of a potential therapist about their experience with brief therapy. There is debate within the field, but many agree that brief therapy is more difficult than open-ended therapy. The reason is that the therapist must be just as knowledgeable and skilled in the ways of the longer-term therapy, but needs additional skills unique to brief therapy. Generally, the brief therapist will be more active, but not necessarily more directive (telling you what to do). The brief psychotherapist also needs to have skill in rapid assessment, or determining the problem and how to facilitate changing it. Furthermore, maintaining a clear therapy focus, as well as a goal or small set of goals is an essential component of brief therapy.

Is brief therapy as effective as longer-term therapies? Well, first we need to define what is "brief." Brief used to be 20-40 sessions when it began. That timeframe is no longer considered brief. Most brief therapists today define a brief treatment duration as 8-20 sessions. Much research suggests that time-limited therapy can be as effective as longer-term therapy (Koss & Butcher, 1986; Malan, 1976; Strupp & Binder, 1984). The question as to whether those changes last as long as those in longer-term therapy has yet to be answered. But the metaphor many brief therapists adhere to is the medical doctor who does not spend time figuring out how to fix the patient's immune system, but rather cures illness and injury as they come up throughout the patient's life. This model is called "brief, intermittent psychotherapy throughout the life-cycle" (Cummings, 1988) and is popular among brief therapists. Once again, the approach you take toward solving your problem(s) and engaging in personal growth is entirely one of personal choice.

Some theorists in brief therapy whose names you may hear are:
• Davanloo—Intensive Short-Term Dynamic Psychotherapy (ISTDP)
• Mann—Time Limited Psychotherapy
• Wolberg—Flexible Short-Term Psychotherapy
• Bellak—Intensive Brief and Emergency Psychotherapy
• Sifneos—Short-Term Anxiety Provoking Therapy
• Bloom—Focused Single-Session Therapy
• Klerman—Interpersonal Psychotherapy
    (Bloom, 1992)

In addition, Malan, Strupp and Binder, and the cognitive-behavioral or behavioral therapies mentioned earlier, are also brief models of psychotherapy.

Psychological Testing

Psychological testing is important to mention since you may be looking for this service as well as psychotherapy. Psychological testing is useful for many purposes. These reasons include:

• To better understand an individual's personality
• Intelligence testing; IQ and cognitive (thinking) functioning
• Effective treatment planning

- Assessing learning disabilities (LDs)
- Assessing possible attention deficit disorder (ADD with/out Hyperactivity)
- Gaining accurate information on a child's development
- Assessing possible brain dysfunction or injury
- Determining how "fit" a person is for psychotherapy, and how to help the person best if therapy is deemed not helpful for him/her
- Lending information in legal proceedings such as child custody, competency to stand trial, possible insanity (a legal criteria, *not* a psychological one), predicting dangerous behavior
- Diagnostic clarity

Psychologists perform psychological testing, and although Master's level clinicians may administer and even score psychological tests, many states require that a licensed psychologist who is ultimately responsible and accountable for the results interpret the tests. This means that while doctoral trainees give much testing throughout schooling, the results are carefully proof-read, edited and confirmed by a supervisor who is a licensed psychologist.

Additionally, different types of psychologists provide different types of testing. Almost all clinical psychologists are trained in personality, intelligence, and psychodiagnostic testing. Child psychologists will have experience in developmental testing on children of ages varying from a few weeks old through adolescence, as well as attention deficit hyperactivity disorder (ADHD) and learning disability (LD) testing. Forensic psychologists (integration of psychology and the law) give psychological tests for competency to stand trial, insanity (used in less than 1% of criminal cases, and is a successful defense only 1-10% of the time it is employed), child custody and other psychological issues related to the law. Neuropsychologists, whose training is in how brain function and behavior are related, are exceptionally well trained at giving tests sensitive to brain dysfunction or damage and how it would affect a person's behavior. Very often neuropsychologists are also experienced with ADHD and LD assessment. The testing neuropsychologists provide is different from that of neurologists who are medical doctors. The neurological assessment is focused more on nervous system functioning and less on behavior, although behavior is still a component. If you are looking for psychological testing for yourself, a relative or child, it is best to contact a psychologist who can do the testing or refer you to a more specific and appropriate professional who can.

CHAPTER 6: SUBSPECIALTY AREAS

Subspecialty areas is the third pillar of psychotherapy worth noting. Subspecialty areas refer to particular problems in which a psychotherapist may have more experience, interest and training, such as anxiety, depression, eating disorders, childhood trauma, victims of violence, substance abuse, grief and loss, relationship issues, sexual orientation confusion, sexual dysfunction, phobias, childhood bedwetting, and a vast array of other psychological difficulties.

What has been addressed thus far is theoretical orientation and type of psychotherapy. As an example, say you start your search for a therapist by talking to a psychotherapist whose general theoretical orientation is cognitive-behavioral, and who mostly does child therapy. You are comfortable with her credentials and schooling. But you still need to know about her subspecialty areas. The following question should come to mind: *What is the therapist's knowledge and experience with your child's problem?* Your child may be acting out in school, or s(he) may be having a problem with bedwetting. You need to know if the therapist feels comfortable working with that issue. (By the way, the two examples we have just listed are exceedingly common, and it is likely that any child therapist will have significant experience with these issues.) But other issues may be more complex or less common.

It is most important for a psychotherapist who identifies him/herself as behavioral or cognitive-behavioral to have experience with the particular issues you are bringing to therapy. This is because cognitive-behavioral therapies are based on observable behavior and specific techniques rather than general approaches, and you are going to want someone who has some practice with those techniques. It is less necessary, but still important, for those therapists who have a more insight-oriented approach (any form of psychodynamic or humanistic/existential) to have significant experience with the specific problems you present. That is because many of the underlying assumptions remain the same in the insight-oriented approaches, regardless of your problem. This in no way implies that insight-oriented approaches are less effective.

Remember that a tremendous body of research suggests no differences in the effectiveness of cognitive-behavioral, psychodynamic and humanistic/existential therapies, and that all have been demonstrated to be effective for most persons and problems, with very few exceptions.

Therefore, we suggest that the more technique-oriented a psychotherapist is, the more important it is for that therapist to have experience with your specific problem. Similarly, if you do not have a very specific request, such as dealing with a phobia or obsessive hand-washing, a more insight-oriented approach will serve you well. There are a vast variety of problems for which people seek therapy, as well as dramatic differences in personality that reflect the richness and complexity of humanity. Therefore, psychotherapists employ creativity as well as knowledge and skill to foster change and help you more effectively.

At the end of the chapter, we have given you summary examples of hypothetical psychotherapists' credentials, theoretical orientation, type of therapy practiced, and subspecialty areas in order to make the difficult process of choosing a psychotherapist more manageable.

The following are just some examples of the many different areas in which a psychotherapist may specialize. If you recall from the Introduction chapter, we used the yellow pages of the phone book to illustrate the varying degrees of psychotherapists. Please join us for another tour of the yellow pages to discover which areas psychotherapists may advertise as their area of expertise. (The following is not an exhaustive list, but it does cover the most common subspecialty areas.)

Addictions—This includes any difficulties with alcohol or substance dependence or abuse, dual diagnoses (a substance abuse in conjunction with another primary mental illness), and any emotional or mental difficulties secondary to the alcohol or drug use (such as anxiety induced by hallucinogen use). This area also includes such addictions as gambling addictions, sexual addictions, or addictions to the Internet. Some psychotherapists may choose not to work with all of the addictions, but may focus on one particular disorder (e.g., gambling).

Anxiety Disorders/Panic—This refers to any anxiety difficulties including panic attacks, agoraphobia (fear of crowded places), separation anxiety, generalized anxiety or compulsive worrying, obsessions and/or compulsions, phobias and fears. Post-traumatic stress disorder (PTSD) is mentioned separately from this category because people often will specialize in PTSD as they work with trauma victims, without necessarily treating the other anxiety disorders.

Attention Deficit/Hyperactivity Disorder (ADHD)—This one is obvious. Psychotherapists who treat this often provide the assessment/testing as well as the remediation, which could involve medication, time management, social skills training, etc.

Autism—Psychotherapists who work with autistic individuals will often work with the families as well to help them cope with the difficulties associated with autism.

Career Counseling—This type of counseling is most often found in university counseling centers, but can also be found in the community. Individuals who provide career counseling may provide testing, exploration of interests and talents, and help in the career search.

Depression—This specialty area can include any of the depressive disorders including major depression (sometimes referred to as clinical depression) and manic depression (or bipolar disorder). These psychotherapists will work with any of the associated difficulties including cognitive impairment (concentration problems), suicidal thoughts, low self-esteem, poor energy, and sleep difficulties.

Eating Disorders/issues/concerns—This area covers bulimia, anorexia nervosa, overeating, compulsive eating, binge eating, and body image concerns.

Impulse control disorders—Psychotherapists working with these disorders may work with kleptomania (compulsive stealing), pyromania (fire-setting), and trichotillomania (compulsive hair pulling).

Learning Disabilities—Similar to ADHD, psychotherapists who work with the learning disabled may provide testing, remediation, or both.

Marital/Partner Difficulties—This area refers to any type of marital problems, such as communication difficulties, unfaithfulness, and lack of trust. These psychotherapists may also work with some of the other categories covered here, such as sexual dysfunction and spousal abuse, as these issues are often the precursors to a couple seeking counseling.

Post-Traumatic Stress Disorder (PTSD)—Some psychotherapists who treat PTSD work exclusively with war veterans, while others work with victims of other types of trauma, including victims of sexual assaults, incest, rape, and violence.

Schizophrenia—This specialty area refers to the work done with individuals suffering from schizophrenia and their families.

Sexual Dysfunction/Sexual Disorders—This is a broad area that covers a wide range of difficulties, including inability to achieve orgasm or sustain an erection, low sex drive, painful intercourse, or premature ejaculation. It also refers to problems like fetishes, voyeurism, exhibitionism, frotteurism (being sexually aroused by rubbing against a non-consenting person), and sado-masochism.

Sexuality—This area refers to those individuals who are questioning their sexuality, or who already identify themselves as gay, lesbian, or bisexual but are trying to deal with difficulties associated with coming out or being gay. This specialty also refers to those individuals who are struggling with their gender identity, or may be considering a gender-change operation.

Sexual Offenders—Psychotherapists who work with sexual offenders work with perpetrators of sexual assaults and rapes, including those who assault children (pedophiles).

Sleep Disorders—The sleep disorders include a number of sleep difficulties, such as insomnia, nightmares, sleepwalking, narcolepsy (falling asleep unexpectedly during the day), and extreme fatigue.

Spousal Abuse/Violence/Anger Management—These psychotherapists work with perpetrators of violence or those who recognize they have difficulty controlling their anger. The violent offenders are often court-ordered to treatment, but many do seek treatment voluntarily.

Stress Management/Relaxation—This area can include any type of relaxation work, which may or may not involve hypnosis.

Illustrations

Example 1

Training:
    Doctoral program –   Fully accredited by American Psychological Association (APA)

    Predoctoral internship -   Fully accredited by APA
Credentials: Psy.D. - psychology
    M.S. - psychology
License or certification: Licensed clinical psychologist
Theoretical orientation: Humanistic/existential (primary)
    Object relations, self psychology (secondary)
    Training in cognitive-behavioral techniques (secondary)
Types of therapy practiced: Individual, group
    Couples (secondary); family (secondary)
Subspecialty areas: Eating issues and body image concerns, relationship difficulties, depression, anxiety, adjustment and transition, victims of violence, psychological testing

Specific training/experience in brief therapy: Yes

Example 2

Training:	
Master's program –	Fully accredited by Council on Social Work Education (CSWE)
Credentials:	M.S.W.
License or certification:	Licensed clinical social worker (LICSW)
Theoretical orientation:	Psychodynamic (primary)
	Behavioral (secondary)
Types of therapy practiced:	Child play, adolescent talk
	Family and individual adult (secondary)
Subspecialty areas:	Bedwetting, school refusal, marital conflict, eating problems, children of divorce, academic difficulties, testing for learning disabilities and attention deficit disorder
Specific training/experience in brief therapy:	No

CHAPTER 7: CHOOSING A PSYCHOTHERAPIST

In this chapter, we will discuss the "how to" of choosing a therapist, based on what you have learned about accreditation, credentialing and licensing, the different kinds of psychotherapists, and the three pillars of psychotherapy. You will be guided through specific questions that will be important for you to ask a prospective psychotherapist, and given many tips and suggestions related to that topic. But before we do that, let us discuss what you need to do before you even pick up the phone.

Know Thyself

Having all the necessary information is important, but if you do not know what you want and how you work best, it's useless. Now would be a good time to refer back to the worksheet you completed towards the beginning of the book. Remember the three pillars we have discussed:

- Theoretical orientation
- Types of therapy
- Subspecialty areas

It is helpful to have a clear idea of what type of psychotherapy (child, adult, group, individual, family, couples) and what subspecialty (eating problems, depression, anxiety, relationship difficulties, general malaise etc.) would best meet your needs before beginning your search. In other words:

Have a request.

You want to be able to explain what you are looking for so you can get the best match for yourself. If you are unsure about what type of therapy would work best, such as individual or group psychotherapy, then ask when you call. More awareness of what would be helpful to you will make it easier for you to find the "best fit." Here is a simple example of how you may want to open a conversation with a prospective psychotherapist:

I am looking to get my son into psychotherapy. He is seven years old and has been wetting his bed at night for the past eighteen months. I am aware that various types of therapy are out there, like play therapy and group therapy, and I was hoping I could ask you some questions.

This is quick and conveys a lot of information, including the age of the person (seven), the type of therapy requested (child) and a brief description of the problem (bedwetting or enuresis). It also lets the therapist know that you know a little something about it. The therapist will then be able to zone in more precisely, and ask you appropriate questions as well as answer yours.

Reflect on what theoretical orientation or approach you think would work best for you.

Keep in mind that the therapist's personal style and personality will affect your comfort with that therapist, so put slightly less weight on theoretical orientation. We do not recommend that you begin by asking about *theoretical orientation*. The reason for this is that most psychotherapists are reluctant to share that information until they know more about your situation. This is in no way underhanded. Most psychotherapists have many tools to draw upon in helping a person in psychotherapy. Therefore, a psychotherapist is going to want to assess a problem a bit more thoroughly before committing to an approach that may or may not work for you. But if you ask the question a bit later in the dialogue, you are more likely to get a more specific answer.

Reflect on the values (if any) that are important to you in a psychotherapist

In addition, spend some time thinking about values that are important to you, and whether these values will have an impact on your decision in choosing a psychotherapist. For instance, do you have strong religious beliefs that relate to what you would like to work on? Some therapists are exceptionally good at integrating issues of faith into psychotherapy. What about cultural differences? What would be potential obstacles or possible benefits to seeing a psychotherapist of a different gender or cultural background? Is it relevant for you? Is it important that your therapist be homosexual or heterosexual? Think about it.

Research and experience suggest that most of the time differences or similarities in gender, culture, sexual orientation, age, race and other individual differences do not have a significant negative impact on psychotherapy. Nevertheless, if you have strong feelings or beliefs about particular values or qualities you would like in a therapist, it could have a negative impact and you may want to ask. Psychotherapists vary in how comfortable they are divulging personal information. Do not be offended if a therapist is reluctant to share. After all, that therapist does not know how that information will impact the person with whom s(he) has just made contact. So you need to feel it out for yourself and determine how comfortable you are knowing or not knowing.

Reflect on your comfort level regarding training.

Spend time thinking about how comfortable you are with various types of training. We have provided detailed information regarding many different training models and degree requirements. Do you feel more comfortable with a doctoral-level psychotherapist? Would you rather see a person trained solely in marriage and family psychotherapy as opposed to a generalist trained in marriage and family as well as other types of therapy? Do you want a briefer model of therapy, or are you more interested in longer-term work and deeper understanding?

You should now have some sense of what you are looking for and what you will find comfortable. This brings us to the most important part of choosing your psychotherapist.

You must feel comfortable with and like your psychotherapist.

One of the more significant indicators of positive psychotherapy outcome is a person's like, comfort, and respect for his or her psychotherapist. It is essential that you keep this in mind as you make your phone calls. What is also important to remember is that a psychotherapy session is not a "normal" one-to-one interaction, and is different from most other types of relationships in our culture. For this reason, everyone experiences some discomfort for the first few meetings of psychotherapy. You need to tease apart discomfort due to the situation, and discomfort due to feelings you have about your psychotherapist.

So in summary:

---

1. Have a request.

2. Reflect on what theoretical orientation or approach you think would work best for you.

3. Reflect on the values that are important to you in a psychotherapist.

4. Reflect on your comfort level regarding training.

5. Remember that you must feel comfortable with and like your psychotherapist.

Where to go

There are many places you can go to find help. We have provided many sources of support in the Resources chapter (Chapter 8). Generally though, you may contact any of the following when seeking psychotherapy:

- Local associations (i.e. county or city mental health association) for referrals
- State or national mental health associations for referrals
- Community mental health centers (CMHC's)
- Private psychotherapy agencies
- Individual psychotherapy practitioners
- Hospitals
- Private psychiatric or residential facilities (many have both inpatient and outpatient therapy)
- Local support groups
- Local universities/colleges which may have psychotherapy clinics or mental health centers

If you feel you are at risk of hurting yourself or someone else, please seek services immediately. You can call the emergency room of any hospital, or 9-1-1. It's also a good idea to tell a close friend, relative or other support person as well.

Making the calls

You have previously been given a concise example of an "opener" when calling a prospective therapist, providing you a foundation for more detailed and incisive questions. Generally, you want to ask open-ended questions as opposed to closed-ended questions. For instance, "What is your experience doing therapy with children," will get a more thorough answer than, "Do you have a lot of experience working with children," in which the answer will be a simple "Yes," or "No."

So you have just finished saying"...*and I was wondering if I could ask you some questions,*" to which you hopefully got a positive response, or at least a response such as, "I can not really talk now, but I could at [such-and-such time]." It is suggested that you continue from there with the following:

Question 1: *What is your experience with [type of psychotherapy—child, family, group, individual, couples, psychological testing]?*

When you ask this question, you will likely get an explanation of how long the psychotherapist has been doing that type of psychotherapy. But you may also get information about subspecialties. Obviously, if that information covers what you are looking for, you need not ask Question 3.

Question 2: *Would you mind telling me about your training and credentials?*

You will want to phrase the question this way because some psychotherapists may feel a bit defensive when asked. Most will not, and will answer freely if asked. But some might feel you are questioning their ability, skill or experience. You may be, in fact, be questioning these things, and that is an appropriate area for you to explore. You do not know the prospective psychotherapist, and need to know if s(he) has adequate training and credentials with which you are comfortable. Most psychotherapists understand that a client who asks such questions is simply concerned with helping him or herself.

Please refer to Chapters 2 and 3 for more information about the credentials your prospective psychotherapist provides. If you cannot find the information in this guide, ask the therapist; i.e. "I'm not familiar with that degree. What accrediting body is that under? Is that a Master's or Doctoral degree?" etc. Both of us have answered such questions, and appreciate that clients care enough about their psychological care to ask.

Question 3: *What is your experience with [problem you'd like to work on]?*

You ask this question to assess subspecialty areas. But many psychotherapists are experienced with a wide range of problems. If you are getting a good feeling from the psychotherapist and are comfortable with the way you are relating, do not jump the gun and end the dialogue if the person seems less experienced with your specific problem. But if you do not hear your request in the psychotherapist's listed subspecialties, ask anyway. Maybe the therapist used to be involved in that area, but does less of it now, or that many people are put-off by stating s(he) specializes in a certain area; i.e. sexual dysfunction. There are many possibilities why your problem area was not mentioned even if the therapist is experienced with it. Following up will help you get the details you need.

Question 4: What would you say is your major theoretical orientation?

First of all, most psychotherapists will be impressed that you are familiar with the phrase "theoretical orientation." Secondly, most psychotherapists will likely answer this question by stating that they are "eclectic." There are two ways of being eclectic:

- Structural eclecticism—A therapist applies certain approaches and techniques based on the problem with which the client is presenting.
- Integrative psychotherapy—A blend of approaches used somewhat simultaneously.

Some research suggests that up to 80% of psychotherapists identify themselves as eclectic. However, most psychotherapists are grounded in some form of psychodynamic, cognitive-behavioral or humanistic/existential theory. You'll probably need a follow-up question to the answer of "eclectic," such as:

What approaches or theorists are you most influenced by?

Remember that many psychotherapists will remain uncomfortable answering because they will want to know more about you and how to help you before committing to a specific approach. If you can simply get a general idea, it will be helpful. If you explain more about what you are looking for, and some of your ideas on what you think might be helpful to you, this will likely lead to a more productive dialogue about the therapist's theoretical orientation. For instance, if you are struggling with panic attacks and feel that a very focused technique and task oriented-approach could be helpful, say so and see if you get a response you are comfortable with. In this scenario, cognitive-behavioral therapy will be most congruent with these needs and desired approach. If you are more interested in general insights about "the way you are," say so, and see what kind of response you get. We have included space for you to write in the *buzz-names* and *buzz-words* your prospective therapist may use during this dialogue. This will give you a better indication of their theoretical orientation and what to expect from them during therapy.

Question 5: *What is your experience or training in brief psychotherapy [if desired]?*

Brief psychotherapy has become much more prominent in the past twenty-five or so years. This means that practitioners who are in their 40's or younger are more likely to have training/education in brief therapy. This is not to say that older psychotherapists will not be experienced or adept at brief therapy, but likely do not have formalized training. This question is obviously only for those who are interested in time-limited therapy. If you are, and you get an encouraging answer to this question, follow up with:

What is your more specific theoretical approach in brief therapy?

Refer to the list of brief therapist names and therapies in the latter part of the "types of psychotherapy" chapter (Chapter 5).

Question 6: *What is your fee?*

Most psychotherapists and agencies with psychotherapists have sliding scales. This means that they adjust their fees depending on your financial situation. You need to talk with them about that in order to determine if the fee scale is acceptable to you. Compare fees if you like, but remember that quality is essential when it comes to mental health care. Furthermore, it is usually best to discuss this with the psychotherapist if it is a private practice. Often there are office managers who handle matters such as fees, but if the therapist has a feel for your situation, s(he) may be more likely to consider your request. If the fee seems high, do not end the conversation. Sometimes things can be done. *See Question 8*—it is a very important one.

Question 7: Are you a provider for [your insurance plan]?

The reason for this question is obvious. But we want to make it clear that you are *not* necessarily restricted to mental health providers who take your insurance, or those who are providers under your HMO. We will discuss this in detail as we continue this chapter. *So if the psychotherapist is not a provider under your insurance, or does not take your insurance, it is not the end of the road, particularly if you are becoming comfortable with the psychotherapist. Once again, see Question 8.*

Question 8: If I were to pay out-of-pocket, could a reduced fee be worked out?

We cannot emphasize enough how important this question is. As the trend of most insurance companies and HMO's is to further limit the amount of money allocated for mental health annually, the number of psychotherapy visits in a psychotherapy regimen has been drastically cut over the past twenty-five years. Many insurance companies allocate approximately $500 per year, which usually allows no more than six sessions.

However, insurance companies and HMO's also generally require much paperwork to be done by the psychotherapist, including detailed documentation of treatment. Many therapists feel constricted by this, and you may feel as though your confidentiality is not as secure as you prefer. In addition, you might feel limited by the choices of therapists given to you by your insurance plan. Clients, along with psychotherapists, often try to reduce these problems by arranging an out-of-pocket fee, and you might want to pursue that route. This is a very common practice, and one that is coming back into fashion as consumers (clients) and providers (medical doctors, psychologists etc.) feel increasingly burdened by the managed care industry.

Some psychotherapists would rather take a lower fee in order to avoid significant paperwork, client confidentiality issues (having to reveal too much information to the insurer), and possible time and session constraints imposed by a particular insurance company. So if you are willing to do this, it will give you and your psychotherapist greater freedom in your psychotherapy.

Question 9: *[Any question(s) related to values important to you.]*

Because this is the first conversation you have ever had with this person, it is recommended that you save personal questions that are important to you until the first face-to-face meeting. However, some value-related questions could be asked in this first phone contact, such as whether or not the therapist speaks a particular language, or if s(he) ever spent time in a country in which you grew up. But if you determine that religion, sexual orientation or other often sensitive topics are important enough to affect your psychotherapy, it is recommended to let this go until you and your prospective therapist feel a little more comfortable with one another. You are likely to get a more straightforward answer this way.

Intuition, intuition, intuition

Intuition is very important in choosing a psychotherapist. Go with your gut, keeping in mind that your gut may feel a little odd simply because of the uniqueness of the situation. Keep in mind:

How you think and feel about your psychotherapist will have a significant impact on the success of your psychotherapy.

So you must exercise some of the skill that psychotherapists use. This means paying attention to both the content and the process while having your initial phone conversation. Content is the information you will be getting as a result of the questions you ask. But just as important is the process of your interaction, and how it feels to you. This is what psychotherapists reflect on all day while in session with clients. They pay attention to both the content of what a client is saying and the process or what is going on while it is being said. You must do this too. It's actually kind of fun and will provide you with a tremendous amount of material when both are taken together. *Remember that psychotherapists are people too.* This means they have bad days, may feel irritable or hurried at a particular moment, and do not enjoy being insulted any more than anyone else. So be a smart consumer, but a considerate one as well.

It will not be helpful to you to come across as critical or judgmental, and therapists will likely respond like everyone else with defensiveness to such an attitude. Remember that the prospective therapist wants to help you and you want to receive help. In other words, you are on the same team and you are assessing if your game plans match.

A NOTE ABOUT THE SELECTION FORMS

The following form is for your use. It is intended to be a guide for interviewing prospective psychotherapists, so feel free to take notes and scribble as you see fit. We have supplied you with four of these blank forms. If you think you will need more, feel free to photocopy the forms for your use. In fact, we hope you do use as many of these sheets as necessary to make your search easier and more effective.

PSYCHOTHERAPIST SELECTION FORM

Question 1: **What is your experience with [type of psychotherapy—child, family, group, individual, couples, psychological testing]?**

Question 2: **Would you mind telling me about your training and credentials?**

Question 3: **What is your experience with [problem you'd like to work on]?**

Question 4: **What would you say is your major theoretical orientation?**
(Follow-up, if necessary) What approaches or theorists are you most influenced by?

      Buzz-names _____

      Buzz-words _____

Question 5: **What is your experience or training in brief psychotherapy [if desired]?**
(Follow-up) What is your more specific theoretical approach in brief therapy?

Question 6: **Generally, what is your fee?**
(See Question 8 if it seems too high for you.)

      $ _____

Question 7: **What insurance do you accept?**
(See Question 8 if therapist does not accept your insurance.)

Question 8: **If I were to pay out-of-pocket, could a reduced fee be worked out?**
(Follow-up) What would be your fee range?

Yes _____ *No* _____

$ _____

Question 9: *[Any question(s) related to values important to you.]*

PSYCHOTHERAPIST SELECTION FORM

Question 1: **What is your experience with [type of psychotherapy—child, family, group, individual, couples, psychological testing]?**

Question 2: **Would you mind telling me about your training and credentials?**

Question 3: **What is your experience with [problem you'd like to work on]?**

Question 4: **What would you say is your major theoretical orientation?** *(Follow-up, if necessary) What approaches or theorists are you most influenced by?*

     Buzz-names _____

     Buzz-words _____

Question 5: **What is your experience or training in brief psychotherapy [if desired]?** *(Follow-up) What is your more specific theoretical approach in brief therapy?*

Question 6: **Generally, what is your fee?** *(See Question 8 if it seems too high for you.)*

     $ _____

Question 7: **What insurance do you accept?**
(See Question 8 if therapist does not accept your insurance.)

Question 8: **If I were to pay out-of-pocket, could a reduced fee be worked out?**
(Follow-up) What would be your fee range?

Yes _____ No _____

$ _____

Question 9: ***[Any question(s) related to values important to you.]***

PSYCHOTHERAPIST SELECTION FORM

Question 1: What is your experience with [type of psychotherapy—child, family, group, individual, couples, psychological testing]?

Question 2: Would you mind telling me about your training and credentials?

Question 3: What is your experience with [problem you'd like to work on]?

Question 4: What would you say is your major theoretical orientation? (Follow-up, if necessary) What approaches or theorists are you most influenced by?

Buzz-names _____

Buzz-words _____

Question 5: What is your experience or training in brief psychotherapy [if desired]? (Follow-up) What is your more specific theoretical approach in brief therapy?

Question 6: Generally, what is your fee? (See Question 8 if it seems too high for you.)

$ _____

Question 7: *What insurance do you accept?*
(See Question 8 if therapist does not accept your insurance.)

Question 8: *If I were to pay out-of-pocket, could a reduced fee be worked out?*
(Follow-up) What would be your fee range?

Yes _____ *No* _____

$ _____

Question 9: *[Any question(s) related to values important to you.]*

PSYCHOTHERAPIST SELECTION FORM

Question 1: *What is your experience with [type of psychotherapy—child, family, group, individual, couples, psychological testing]?*

Question 2: *Would you mind telling me about your training and credentials?*

Question 3: *What is your experience with [problem you'd like to work on]?*

Question 4: *What would you say is your major theoretical orientation? (Follow-up, if necessary) What approaches or theorists are you most influenced by?*

Buzz-names _____

Buzz-words _____

Question 5: *What is your experience or training in brief psychotherapy [if desired]? (Follow-up) What is your more specific theoretical approach in brief therapy?*

Question 6: *Generally, what is your fee? (See Question 8 if it seems too high for you.)*

$ _____

Question 7: **What insurance do you accept?**
(See Question 8 if therapist does not accept your insurance.)

Question 8: **If I were to pay out-of-pocket, could a reduced fee be worked out?**
(Follow-up) What would be your fee range?

Yes _____ *No* _____

$ _____

Question 9: *[Any question(s) related to values important to you.]*

CHAPTER 8: RESOURCES

ALCOHOL AND DRUG ABUSE

General Information

American Council for Drug Education (ACDE)
www.acde.org   800-488-DRUG
    ACDE is a national, nonprofit organization that works to educate the public in drug abuse prevention through pamphlets, films, and broadcast media. ACDE provides educational programs and materials to help parents, educators, and professionals.

National Clearinghouse for Alcohol and Drug Information (NCADI)
www.health.org   800-729-6686; 800-487-4889 (TTY/TDD)
    NCADI is an information clearinghouse and is part of the Center for Substance Abuse Prevention. NCADI provides public educational materials for an inexpensive fee and access to prevention, intervention and treatment resources.

National Council on Alcoholism and Drug Dependence (NCADD)
www.ncadd.org   800-NCA-CALL
    NCADD is a nonprofit agency that works towards public education, advocacy, and changing legislation. NCADD also brought attention to the special needs of women, ethnic groups, and lesbians and gay men. The organization produces public service announcements, educational pamphlets, fact sheets, and sponsors conferences. It also sponsors National Alcohol Awareness Month.

National Drug and Alcohol Treatment Referral Service 800-662-HELP
    This service provides educational materials, as well as referrals to treatment programs including Al-Anon, AA and NA.

Resources for the Addict

Alcohol and Drug Abuse Hotline   **800-ALCOHOL**
This national, toll-free hotline makes referrals to treatment providers across the nation for alcoholics and drug addicts.

Alcoholics Anonymous (AA)
www.alcoholics-anonymous.org   **212-870-3400**
AA is a spiritual self-help program based on the Twelve Steps. There are no fees to join AA, and anyone can join who wishes to stop drinking. There are meetings sponsored throughout the world every day of the year. Locally sponsored groups can be found in the phone book or by contacting the AA world services office listed above.

Cocaine Anonymous (CA)
www.ca.org   **310-559-5833**
Cocaine Anonymous is a support group for cocaine addicts based on the Twelve Steps of AA. Locally sponsored groups can be found in the phone book or by contacting the CA world services office listed above.

Cocaine Hotline   **800-COCAINE**
1-800-COCAINE, a public service of Phoenix House, is a 24-hour toll-free hotline that provides information about cocaine and cocaine addiction and provides referrals to treatment providers across the nation.

Narcotics Anonymous (NA)
www.na.org   **800-777-1515; 818-773-9999**
NA is a self-help program for drug addicts based on the Twelve Steps of AA. Membership includes people addicted to a wide range of both illegal and prescription drugs. Locally sponsored groups can be found in the found book or by contacting the NA world services office listed above.

Nicotine Anonymous (NicA)   877-879-4762; 415-750-0328

NicA is a self-help program based on the Twelve Steps of AA. NicA sponsors weekly meetings in several states across the country. Membership is free, but donations are accepted at the end of each meeting. Locally sponsored groups can be found in the phone book or by contacting the NicA world services office listed above.

Treatment Resources for the Deaf

National Deaf Education Network and Clearinghouse
clerccenter.gallaudet.edu   202-651-5340 (TTY)

This organization publishes a directory of alcohol and drug treatment programs for the deaf across the United States.

Substance and Alcohol Intervention Services for the Deaf (SAISD)
www.rit.edu/~257www   585-475-4978 (voice & TTY)

SAISD, located in Rochester, NY, sponsors support groups, conducts interventions, and provides educational information to the public. SAISD also consults with programs across the country to help them improve services for the deaf.

Treatment Resources for Ethnic Minorities

Indian Health Service (IHS)
www.ihs.gov   301-443-2038

IHS provides information on intervention and prevention for chemically dependent Native Americans and Alaskan Natives. IHS oversees twelve regional offices across the country. Referrals to treatment providers can be obtained by contacting the IHS regional office in your area.

National Alliance for Hispanic Health
www.hispanichealth.org   202-387-5000; 866-SU-FAMILIA
The National Alliance for Hispanic Health is a network of health and human service providers servicing the Hispanic community on a variety of health issues. It also operates a toll-free helpline that provides health information and referrals.

National Asian Pacific American Families Against Substance Abuse (NAPAFASA)
www.napafasa.org   212-625-5795
NAPAFASA, Inc. is a national organization that works towards public education and prevention of alcohol and drug problems in the Asian and Pacific Islander populations. This organization also serves as a national clearinghouse for other Asian Pacific agencies.

National Black Alcoholism and Addictions Council (NBAC)
www.borg.com/~nbac   202-296-2696
NBAC, Inc. is a nonprofit organization that works for public education of alcoholism among African Americans. This organization also provides workshops to treatment providers and the community.

Resources for Families and Friends

Adult Children of Alcoholics (ACA)
www.adultchildren.org   310-534-1815
ACA is a self-help organization based on the Twelve Steps of AA. This organization is open to adults who grew up in alcoholic families. Locally sponsored groups can be found by contacting the ACA at the number listed above.

Al-Anon-Alateen World Directory   **800-344-2666; 888-4AL-ANON**
Al-Anon Family Group Headquarters   **757-563-1600**
www.al-anon.org or www.Al-Anon-Alateen.org

Al-Anon is the largest self-help group for families of alcoholics. Al-Anon/Alateen are nonprofit, self-help organizations based on the Twelve Steps of AA. These groups are open to anyone affected by an alcoholic family member. Locally sponsored groups can be found in the phone book or by contacting the Family Group Headquarters listed above.

Families Anonymous (FA)
www.familiesanonymous.org   **800-736-9805**

FA is a self-help group for families of young alcoholics based on the Twelve Steps of AA. FA helps families understand and cope with behavioral problems related to alcoholism. Locally sponsored groups can be found in the phone book or by contacting FA at the number listed above.

Nar-Anon   **310-547-5800**

Nar-Anon is an international self-help organization for families of drug addicts based on the Twelve Steps of AA. Locally sponsored groups can be found in the phone book or by contacting Nar-Anon at the number listed above.

National Association for Children of Alcoholics (NACoA)
www.nacoa.net   **301-468-0985**

NACoA is a national, nonprofit organization advocating for children of alcoholics. It works towards educating the public and serves as a national information clearinghouse.

ToughLove
www.toughlove.org   **215-348-7090**

ToughLove is a support group for parents of chemically dependent youth with behavioral problems. This organization teaches parents new skills in dealing with their children. Locally sponsored groups can be found by contacting ToughLove at the number listed above.

Resources for Gay and Lesbian Addicts

National Association of Lesbian and Gay Addiction Professionals (NALGAP)
www.nalgap.org   **703-465-0539**
NALGAP is a national, nonprofit membership organization that provides information and support for individuals in recovery and professionals working with lesbian/gay/bisexual/transgender communities. NALGAP makes referrals to a network of gay-sensitive treatment providers and also publishes a quarterly newsletter.

Pride Institute
www.pride-institute.com   **800-54-PRIDE**
Pride Institute is an inpatient drug and alcohol treatment program exclusively for lesbians and gay men. Pride follows the Twelve Steps of AA. The program lasts one month and makes referrals for further treatment.

Resources for Professionals in Recovery

Anesthetists in Recovery (AIR)   **800-654-5167**
AIR is a national network that provides support and treatment referrals for nurse anesthetists recovering from chemical dependency.

International Doctors in AA (IDAA)
www.idaa.org   **859-277-9379**
IDAA holds annual meetings for both AA and Al-Anon members, and is open to medical doctors, dentists, psychologists, veterinarians, and medical scientists.

International Lawyers in AA (ILAA)
www.ilaa.org
ILAA holds annual meetings for lawyers in recovery and has several locally sponsored groups.

International Nurses Anonymous (INA)   913-842-3893
INA is a national support group for nurses in any Twelve-Step program. INA has annual meetings.

International Pharmacists Anonymous (IPA)   908-537-4295
IPA is an international network for pharmacists in recovery.

Psychologists Helping Psychologists   703-578-1644
This organization is a national network for psychologists in recovery.

Social Workers Helping Social Workers   515-422-7485
This organization is an international network for MSW professionals and students in recovery that provides support and education and holds annual retreats.

Resource for Women in Recovery

Women for Sobriety, Inc. (WFS)
www.womenforsobriety.org   215-536-8026
WFS is a national network of support groups for women in recovery. All-women groups meet weekly with a focus on current concerns and improving self-esteem, rather than on past drinking behavior. WFS publishes a newsletter and other educational materials.

EATING DISORDERS

National Association of Anorexia Nervosa and Associated Disorders (ANAD)
www.anad.org   847-831-3438
ANAD is a national nonprofit organization that sponsors free support groups throughout the United States, provides treatment referrals, and operates a hotline. ANAD also publishes educational materials and a quarterly newsletter.

National Eating Disorders Association (NEDA)
www.nationaleatingdisorders.org   800-931-2237
NEDA provides information about eating disorders and body image concerns through educational materials and prevention programs. NEDA also makes referrals to treatment centers and support groups across the country.

National Food Addiction Hotline   800-USA-0088
This hotline is open daily from 8 A.M. to 8 P.M. (Eastern Standard Time) and noon to 4 P.M. on weekends. It provides callers with information on food addictions as well as treatment referrals.

Overeaters Anonymous (OA)
www.overeatersanonymous.org   505-891-2664; 310-618-8835
OA is a self-help organization for overeaters based on the Twelve Steps of AA. Groups meet weekly nationwide. Locally sponsored groups can be found in the phone book or by contacting OA at the number listed above.

GAMBLING AND OTHER MONEY ISSUES

Debtors Anonymous (DA)
www.debtorsanonymous.org   781-453-2743
DA is a self-help program based on the Twelve Steps of AA. DA is open to anyone who wishes to avoid getting into unsecured debt. Groups meet

regularly. Locally sponsored groups can be found in the phone book or by contacting DA at the number listed above.

Gam-Anon/Gam-A-Teen
www.gam-anon.org   **718-352-1671**

Gam-Anon/Gam-A-Teen are a support program for friends and family of gamblers based on the Twelve Steps of AA. Groups meet regularly with a focus on coping skills and financial planning. Locally sponsored groups can be found by contacting Gam-Anon at the number listed above.

Gamblers Anonymous (GA)
www.gamblersanonymous.org   **213-386-8789**

GA is a self-help program for gamblers based on the Twelve Steps of AA. Groups meet regularly with a focus on support and learning take responsibility. Locally sponsored groups can be found in the phone book or by contacting GA at the number listed above.

National Council on Problem Gambling, Inc.
www.ncpgambling.org   **800-522-4700**

The National Council on Problem Gambling is a nonprofit organization that provides advocacy, education, and treatment referrals, and operates a 24-hour helpline.

SEXUAL DISORDERS

Sex Addicts Anonymous (SAA)
www.sexaa.org   **800-477-8191**

SAA is a self-help program for sex addicts with a focus on abstaining from compulsive and destructive sexual behaviors. Groups meet regularly nationwide and are comprised of mostly male members. SAA publishes a newsletter and other educational materials.

Sexaholics Anonymous (SA)

www.sa.org   615-331-6230

SA is a self-help program for sex addicts with a focus on abstaining from sex with self or outside the marriage. Groups meet regularly nationwide.

Sex & Love Addicts Anonymous (SLAA)

www.slaafws.org   781-255-8825

SLAA is a self-help program for sex and love addicts with a focus on avoiding addictive relationships and learning to maintain a healthy, committed relationship. Groups meet regularly nationwide.

CHILDREN WITH SPECIAL NEEDS

The Association for the Help of Retarded Children (AHRC)

www.ahrc.org   516-626-1000

AHRC is an organization that provides services for people with developmental disabilities. AHRC advocates for support services and provides financial assistance, clinical services, housing, and public education. Membership is available for an annual fee.

Attention Deficit Information Network (AD-IN)

www.addinfonetwork.com   781-455-9895

AD-IN is a Massachusetts-based nonprofit organization that provides information about Attention Deficit Disorder and makes treatment referrals. AD-IN has a network of chapters that holds support groups throughout the country.

Autism Society of America (ASA)

www.autism-society.org   800-3AUTISM

ASA is a national organization that provides information, public education, advocacy, family support, and treatment referrals to local chapters nationwide. ASA also operates a toll-free information line, publishes a bimonthly newsletter, and sponsors an annual conference.

Children and Adults with Attention Deficit Disorder (CHADD)
www.chadd.org   800-233-4050

CHADD is a national, nonprofit, parent-based organization for people with Attention-Deficit/Hyperactivity Disorder. CHADD provides family support, advocacy, and public education. This organization also sponsors conferences and local chapters.

Learning Disability Association of America (LDA)
www.ldanatl.org   412-341-1515

LDA is a national, nonprofit organization that works towards advocacy and public awareness of learning disabilities. LDA provides information, advocacy training, treatment referrals, and consultation with schools to improve services for the learning disables. This organization also sponsors an annual conference and publishes a newsletter.

National Down Syndrome Congress
www.ndsccenter.org   800-232-NDSC

The National Down Syndrome Congress functions as an information clearinghouse to increase public awareness and education about Down Syndrome. The congress also provides advocacy, support, and referral services, sponsors an annual convention, and publishes a newsletter for members.

National Information Center for Children & Youth with Disabilities (NICHCY)
www.nichcy.org   800-695-0285

NICHCY is a national organization that provides information on disabilities and makes referrals. NICHCY focuses on younger disabled people, from birth to age 22.

National Tuberous Sclerosis Association of America (NTSA)
www.ntsa.org   800-225-6872
NTSA is a national, nonprofit organization that provides support to victims and families and makes referrals to resources and local support groups. NTSA funds research grants, provides public education, and publishes numerous newsletters and educational materials for members for an annual contribution.

Spina Bifida Association of America (SBAA)
www.sbaa.org   800-621-3141
SBAA is a national, nonprofit organization that provides a toll-free information and referral service, sponsors research, provides advocacy, and works to increase public awareness. SBAA also sponsors conferences and publishes a bimonthly newsletter for members for an annual fee.

United Cerebral Palsy Association (UCPA)
www.ucpa.org   800-USA-5UCP
UCP is a national organization that acts as an information and referral service. UCP also provides advocacy, sponsors research, and provides direct services through therapy, support groups, and help with finding jobs.

RESOURCES FOR MENTALLY ILL

Alzheimer's Disease Education and Referral Center (ADEAR)
www.alzheimers.org   800-438-4380
ADEAR is a service of the National Institute on Aging. ADEAR functions as an information and referral service, and has numerous publications.

Anxiety Disorders Association of America (ADAA)
www.adaa.org   301-231-9350
ADAA is a national, nonprofit organization that provides support for people with anxiety disorders through nationwide treatment referrals, increasing

public awareness, and advocating for research. ADAA also sponsors conferences, publishes a quarterly newsletter, and has numerous publications.

National Alliance for the Mentally Ill (NAMI)
www.nami.org   800-950-NAMI

NAMI is a national organization that sponsors support groups nationwide for the mentally ill and their families. NAMI also provides advocacy, sponsors research, and works to increase public awareness of mental illness.

National Depressive and Manic-Depressive Association (NDMDA)
www.ndmda.org   800-82-NDMDA

NDMDA is an organization that provides support for people with depression or manic-depression. NDMDA provides treatment referrals and training, and conducts research. NDMDA also publishes a bimonthly newsletter. Members pay an annual fee.

National Mental Health Services Knowledge Exchange Network (KEN)
www.mentalhealth.org   800-789-2647

KEN is a service of the Center for Mental Health Services (CMHC). KEN is a national clearinghouse that provides information about Federal, State, and local mental health service programs, and advocacy organizations.

Recovery, Inc.
www.recovery-inc.com   312-337-5661

Recovery, Inc. is a support program for people with nervous symptoms and disorders. Recovery sponsors training and conferences. Members meet weekly nationwide to learn how to cope with their symptoms. Members also receive a bimonthly newsletter for an annual fee.

Toastmasters International
www.toastmasters.org   949-858-8255

Toastmasters International is a nonprofit organization that provides support for people trying to overcome the fear of public speaking. Members meet weekly and are provided educational materials, a monthly magazine, instruction, and practice. Toastmasters is for people 18 years and older. Locally sponsored groups can be found on their website or by calling the Chamber of Commerce or the number listed above.

DOMESTIC VIOLENCE

Child Help USA
www.childhelpusa.org   800-4-A-CHILD

Child Help USA operates a national information and referral hotline for child abuse. This program also provides treatment, publishes numerous educational materials, and supports research.

National Clearinghouse on Child Abuse and Neglect
www.calib.com/nccanch   800-394-3366

The National Clearinghouse on Child Abuse and Neglect is a division of the U.S. Department of Health and Human Services. This center provides information to professionals about child abuse issues.

National Coalition Against Domestic Violence
www.ncadv.org   303-839-1852

The National Coalition Against Domestic Violence works to support victims through public education, advocacy, policy development and other prevention efforts.

National Domestic Violence Hotline   800-799-SAFE
800-787-3224 (TDD)

This toll-free hotline provides information and treatment referrals for victims of domestic violence.

National Organization for Victims Assistance (NOVA)
www.try-nova.org   800-TRY-NOVA

NOVA is a national, nonprofit organization that provides support to victims through advocacy, education, and direct services. NOVA also publishes a newsletter and educational materials, and sponsors an annual conference.

National Runaway Hotline   800-231-6946

This 24-hour toll-free hotline provides support and resource referrals to runaways. The hotline also relays messages to families.

National Center for Victims of Crime
www.ncvc.org   202-467-8700

The National Center for Victims of Crime strives to help victims rebuild their lives through public education efforts, advocacy, and providing access to treatment resources.

Parents Anonymous (PA)
www.parentsanonymous.org   800-421-0353

PA is a national crisis intervention program that provides free support groups to parents who are potentially abusive to their children. Groups meet regularly nationwide to teach members how to communicate feelings without violence. PA also offers an information and referral hotline.

SEXUAL ABUSE ISSUES

Rape, Abuse, and Incest National Network (RAINN)
www.rainn.org   800-656-HOPE

RAINN is a nonprofit organization that operates a 24-hour toll-free hot-line for victims of sexual assault. This hotline automatically routes each call to the rape crisis center nearest the victim for counseling and support services.

Survivors of Incest Anonymous (SIA)
www.siawso.org   410-893-3322

SIA is a national self-help program for survivors of incest, pedophilia, and rape. SIA is based on the concepts of AA. Groups meet regularly. SIA also sponsors a 24-hour hotline listed above.

HIV, AIDS, & SEXUALLY TRANSMITTED DISEASES

National Prevention Information Network (NPIN)
www.cdcnpin.org   800-458-5231

The National Prevention Information Network is a service of the Centers for Disease Control (CDC). NPIN is a clearinghouse that provides information about HIV/AIDS and STDs regarding prevention, education, and research issues. The center also offers treatment and resource referrals and publishes numerous educational materials.

National AIDS Hotline   800-342-AIDS; 800-344-SIDA(Spanish)
800-243-7889(TTY)

The National AIDS Hotline is a 24-hour hotline run by the Centers for Disease Control. This hotline provides information about AIDS and makes referrals to treatment providers and support groups nationwide.

National STD Hotline　　　　　　　　　　　　　　　**800-227-8922**

The National STD Hotline is operated by the Centers for Disease Control and is available Monday-Friday 8am-11pm.

RESOURCES FOR LESBIANS AND GAYS

Gay and Lesbian National Hotline
www.glnh.org　　　　　　　　　　　　　　　　　　**888-843-4564**

The Gay and Lesbian National Hotline is a national, nonprofit organization that provides peer counseling, information, and treatment referrals. The hotline is open Monday-Friday 6pm-10pm and Saturday noon-5pm EST

National Gay and Lesbian Task Force
www.ngltf.org　　　　　　　　　　　　　　　　　　**202-332-6483**

The National Gay and Lesbian Task Force is a national civil rights organization that works to strengthen gay and lesbian movements at the state and local levels. The task force also serves as the national resource center for grassroots organizations.

Parents, Families and Friends of Lesbians and Gays (PFLAG)
www.pflag.org　　　　　　　　　　　　　　　　　　**202-467-8180**

PFLAG is a grassroots organization that works to increase public awareness of lesbian and gay issues and advocate for better public policy. PFLAG also sponsors conferences, publishes a quarterly newsletter, and offers numerous educational publications. PFLAG has locally sponsored groups that meet nationwide.

PROFESSIONAL ORGANIZATIONS

The following list contains both mental health organizations and accrediting institutions. Some of the mental health organizations may provide referrals to providers in your local area. See Chapter 3 for descriptions of the accrediting institutions.

Accreditation Council for Graduate Medical Education (ACGME)
www.acgme.org   312-464-4920
ACGME is the accrediting body for medical residencies.

American Association for Marriage and Family Therapy (AAMFT)
www.aamft.org   202-452-0109
AAMFT is the national membership organization for marriage and family therapists. It also houses COAMFTE, the accrediting body for marriage and family therapy education.

American Counseling Association
www.counseling.org   800-347-6647
The American Counseling Association is the national membership organization for counselors.

American Psychiatric Association (APA)
www.psych.org   888-357-7924
The American Psychiatric Association is the national membership organization for psychiatrists.

American Psychoanalytic Association (APsaA)
www.apsa.org   212-752-0450
APsaA is a national membership organization for psychoanalysts.

American Psychological Association (APA)
www.apa.org   800-374-2721
APA is the accrediting body for doctoral training programs in psychology. It is also the national membership association for psychologists.

Council for Accreditation of Counseling and Related Educational Programs (CACREP)

www.counseling.org   800-347-6647

CACREP is the accrediting body for counselor education programs.

Council on Social Work Education (CSWE)

www.cswe.org   703-683-8080

CSWE is the accrediting body for social work education programs.

International Association for Analytical Psychology

www.iaap.org   708-475-4848

The International Association for Analytical Psychology is an international membership organization for Jungian analysts.

National Association of School Psychologists (NASP)

www.nasponline.org   301-657-0270

NASP is the national membership organization for school psychologists.

National Association of Social Workers (NASW)

www.naswdc.org   202-408-8600

NASW is the national membership organization for social workers.

National Board for Certified Counselors, Inc. (NBCC)

www.nbcc.org   336-547-0607
                                                                    336-547-0607

Created by the American Counseling Association, NBCC is an independent nonprofit credentialing association for counselors.

National Council for Accreditation of Teacher Education (NCATE)

www.ncate.org   202-466-7496

NCATE is the accrediting body for school psychology training programs.

National League for Nursing (NLN)
www.nln.org   **800-669-1656**
　　NLN is the national membership organization for nurses. It also houses NLNAC, the accrediting body for nursing education.

References—Chapter 3

Accreditation Council for Graduate Medical Education, (1995), *Program Requirements for Residency Education in Psychiatry*

American Psychological Association. (1996), *Graduate Study in Psychology*. Washington, D.C.: American Psychological Association, Inc.

American Psychological Association, (1996), *Guidelines and Principles for Accreditation of Programs in Professional Psychology*

The Commission on Accreditation for Marriage and Family Therapy Education, (1997), *1997 Manual on Accreditation*

The Council for Accreditation of Counseling and Related Educational Programs, (1994), *CACREP Accreditation Standards and Procedures Manual*

Council on Social Work Education, (1994), *Curriculum Policy Statement for Master's Degree Programs in Social Work Education*

National Association of School Psychologists, (1994), *NASP Standards for Training and Field Placement Programs in School Psychology*

National League for Nursing Accrediting Commission, (1997), *Accreditation Manual for Post-Secondary, Baccalaureate and Higher Degree Programs in Nursing*

REFERENCES—CHAPTER 4

Bandura, A. (1977). *Social learning theory.* Englewood Cliffs, NJ: Prentice-Hall.

Beck, A.T., & Weishaar, M.E. (1989). Cognitive therapy. In Corsini, R.J., & Wedding, P. (Eds.), *Current psychotherapies (4th ed.)* (pp. 285-320). Itasca, IL: F.E. Peacock Publishers, Inc.

Beck, A.T. (1972). *Depression: Causes and treatment.* Philadelphia, PA: University of Pennsylvania Press.

Bowlby, J. (1969). *Attachment and loss (v.1).* New York: Basic Books.

Ellis, A. (1989). Rational-emotive therapy. In Corsini, R.J., & Wedding, P. (Eds.), *Current psychotherapies (4th ed.)* (pp.197-239). Itasca, IL: F.E. Peacock Publishers, Inc.

Freud, A. (1936). *The ego and the mechanisms of defense.* New York: International Universities Press.

Herink, R. (Eds.). (1980). *The psychotherapy handbook: The A to Z guide to more that 250 different therapies in use today.* New York: Meridian.

Kohut, H. (1975). *Search for the self.* New York: International Universities Press.

May, R., & Yalom, I. (1989). Existential psychotherapy. In Corsini, R.J., & Wedding, P. (Eds.), *Current psychotherapies (4th ed.)* (pp.363-403). Itasca, IL: F.E. Peacock Publishers, Inc.

Mishne, J.M. (1993). *The Evolution and application of clinical theory: Perspectives from four psychologies.* New York: The Free Press, a Division of Macmillan, Inc.

Mitchell, S.A., & Black, M.J. (1995). *Freud and beyond: A history of modern psychoanalytic thought.* New York: Basic Books.

Patterson, (1973). *Theories of counseling and psychotherapy.* New York: Harper & Row.

Raskin, N.J., & Rogers, C.R. (1989). Client-centered therapy. In Corsini, R.J., & Wedding, P. (Eds.), *Current psychotherapies (4th ed.)* (pp.155-195). Itasca, IL: F.E. Peacock Publishers, Inc.

Rogers, C. R., & Sanford, R.C. (1985). Client-centered psychotherapy. In H.I. Kaplan, B.J. Sadock, & A.M. Friedman (Eds.), *Comprehensive textbook of psychiatry (4th ed.)* (pp.1374-1388). Baltimore, MD: William & Wilkins.

Rychlak, J.F. (1981). *Introduction to personality and psychotherapy: A theory-construction approach (2nd ed.).* Boston, MS: Houghton Mifflin Company.

Skinner, B.F. (1953). *Science and human behavior.* New York: Macmillan.

Sullivan, H.S. (1938). The data of psychiatry. *Schizophrenia as a Human Process.* New York: W.W. Norton.

Yankura, J., & Dryden, W. (1990). *Doing RET: Albert Ellis in action.* New York: Springer Publishing Company, Inc.

Yontef, G.M., & Simkin, J.S. (1989). Gestalt therapy. In Corsini, R.J., & Wedding, P. (Eds.), *Current psychotherapies (4th ed.)* (pp. 323-361). Itasca, IL: F.E. Peacock Publishers, Inc.

References—Chapter 5

Axline, V.M. (1947). *Play therapy: The inner dynamics of childhood.* Boston: Houghton Mifflin.

Bloom, B.L. (1992). *Planned short-term psychotherapy: A clinical handbook.* Boston, MA: Allyn & Bacon.

Bowen, M. (1978). *Family therapy in clinical practice.* New York: Jason Aronson.

Cummings, N.A. (1988). Emergence of the mental health complex: Adaptive and maladaptive responses. *Professional Psychology: Research and Practice, 19,* 308-315.

Dare, C. (1986). Psychoanalytic marital therapy. In N.S. Jacobson, & A.S. Gurman (Eds.), *Clinical handbook of marital therapy* (pp.13-28). New York: Guilford press.

Hanson, J.C., & L'Abate, L. (1982). *Approaches to family therapy.* New York: Macmillan.

Jacobson, N.S., & Holtzworth-Munroe, A. (1986). In N.S. Jacobson, & A.S. Gurman (Eds.), *Clinical handbook of marital therapy* (pp.29-70). New York: Guilford press.

Koss, M.P., & Butcher, J.N. (1986). Research on brief psychotherapy. In A.E. Bergin & S.L. Garfield (Eds.), *Handbook of psychotherapy and behavior change: An empirical analysis (3rd ed.),* pp.627-670. New York: Wiley.

Malan, D.H. (1976). *The frontier of brief psychotherapy: An example of the convergence of research and clinical practice.* New York: Plenum.

Satir, V. (1971). The family as a treatment unit. In J. Haley (ed.), *Changing families, a family therapy reader* (pp.127-133). New York: Grune & Stratton.

Shaffer, J., & Galinski, M.D. (1989). *Models of group therapy (2nd ed.).* Englewood Cliffs, NJ: Prentice Hall.

Strupp, H.H., & Binder, J.L. (1984). *Psychotherapy in a new key: A guide to time-limited dynamic psychotherapy.* New York: Basic Books.

Todd, T.C. (1986). In N.S. Jacobson, & A.S. Gurman (Eds.), *Clinical handbook of marital therapy* (pp.71-106). New York: Guilford press.

Tuma, J.M., & Russ, S.W. (1993). Psychoanalytic psychotherapy with children. In T.R. Kratochwill, & R.J. Morris (Ed.), *Handbook of psychotherapy with children and adolescents* (pp.131-161), Boston, MA: Allyn & Bacon.

Yalom, I. (1985). *The theory and practice of group psychotherapy (3rd ed.).* New York: Basic Books, Inc.

ABOUT THE AUTHORS

Matthew S. Zimmerman, Psy.D. is a licensed psychologist practicing in Fort Lauderdale, Florida. He specializes in eating issues and body image concerns, stress management, relationship issues, and grief and loss. He is currently President-elect of the Broward County Psychological Association, and an adjunct faculty member at Nova Southeastern University's Center for Psychological Studies. Dr. Zimmerman is also involved in classical music as part of the Florida Philharmonic Orchestra and Chorus.

Donna Volpe Strouse, Psy.D. is a licensed psychologist whose specialties include depression, relationship issues, women's issues, personality testing and assessing learning disabilities and attention deficit disorder. She currently works in Information Services at Wellesley College. She resides in Ashland, Massachusetts with her husband Jim, their newborn son Evan, and their dog Yoshi. In her spare time, she enjoys cooking, hiking, snow-shoeing, and most of all, spending time with her family.

0-595-21910-1